Old
Growth

Old Growth

The best writing about trees
from *Orion* magazine

FOREWORD BY
Robin Wall Kimmerer

ILLUSTRATIONS BY
Patrik Svensson

Published by *Orion* magazine.
All essays appeared in *Orion* or *Orion* books except Robin Wall Kimmerer's foreword; "The Coffin Trees," by Jessica J. Lee; and "The Dominion of Roots," by Terese Mailhot.

Orion magazine
1 Short Street
Northampton, MA 01060
www.orionmagazine.org

Editor: Christopher Cox
Editorial Production Manager: Tara Rae Miner
Assistant Editor: Kathleen Yale
Editorial Intern: Juliet Schulman-Hall
Cover and interior illustrations: Patrik Svensson
Designer: Hans Teensma | impressinc.com

This book was made possible by donations from the
Hobson Family Foundation and Josephine Merck.

ISBN: 978-0-913098-02-8

Printed in Canada.

TABLE OF CONTENTS

POEMS

ROOTS

R O B I N W A L L K I M M E R E R

Foreword

I USED TO LIVE in an arboretum. My closest neighbors were
white cedars and a Kentucky coffee tree. The little house by
the prairie in Madison, Wisconsin, was a dream accommoda-
tion for a botany graduate student, in return for the odd bit of
caretaking and rangering on Saturdays.

It was a daily pleasure to wander among the plantings, each
fortuitously bearing a name tag. An arboretum reminds us that there
really is no such thing as just trees—rather, there are firs, birches,
palms, and plums. This book is an arboretum of essays, not showcas-
ing "trees" as a class of beings, but rather stories of interspecies relationships of an arboreal kind, as diverse in scope as trees are in leaf.

A potent and tasty relationship is grounded in food. The University of Wisconsin Arboretum provided me opportunities for
foraging a great range of arboreal abundance, from juneberries to
black walnuts. How generously they share their offspring with us.
The essays in this collection show how working in trees can change
us, as pruning an orchard changed Geronimo Tagatac and making

sugar on a late winter night changed Robin MacArthur.

My duties at the UW Arboretum included wandering about and looking at plants, which I view today as priceless career preparation. In one part of the arboretum, the trees were understood as specimens, arrayed in taxonomic groupings to illustrate the multiplicity of arboreal forms. There are lots of ways to be a tree, variations on a theme of conifer. In his essay "The Things Trees Know," William Bryant Logan speaks of the improvisational nature of tree growth, as akin to a jazz saxophone solo unfolding in response to the changing keys of life.

We don't even have to see them for trees to make a connection with us; sometimes just the scent says "you were here." Deep in the ancient part of the brain that hooks fragrance to memory, we remember things we did not know, like the fleeting scent of cherries evoked by Katrina Vandenberg. My newborn daughter came home from the hospital when the *Tilia americana* was in bloom in the arboretum. I held the blossoms to her nose, thinking that fragrance would assure her she'd come to a good place and imprint trees on her. Her name is Linden.

Near my little house was the horticultural section, the ornamental gardens where in balmy May, the frothy displays of crab apples hovered like pink dawn clouds above the lawn. Lia Purpura's essay on photographing children in trees reminded me of a common occurrence when I lived there: In my ranger capacity, I was often asked to snap photos of smiling families—celebrating new babies or golden anniversaries—framed by flowering branches. I imagine how those photographs, lovingly placed on mantels and grandparents' dressers, continue to elicit smiles at the brides and grooms and coos at the chubby babies.

Once the extravaganza of petals had joined the spent magnolias and fermented on the ground, adorned only by their stamped metal tags with the varietal name and accession number, no one much cared about them anymore. Sometimes that's how trees enter our lives, as a backdrop to our dramas.

Sometimes they are the center of the drama, when a tree becomes more than a representative of its species and expresses itself as an individual, like the heroic bald cypress known as The Senator in Julia Shipley's "The Giving Tree." Sometimes their singularity comes from the hand that planted them. As carriers of memory and life spans that unite human generations, trees become connections to those long gone below the rooting zone, monuments to relationships. Scott Russell Sanders writes of that one beloved buckeye that bound together family, place, and identity. "Trees mark time for the humans who notice them," writes Robert Sullivan of hemlock, which—unthinkably—faces its own demise.

A named tree with great stature at my arboretum, known as the Jackson Oak, has an immense canopy that spreads over swards of Indian grass and blazing star. Alone in the prairie, it has withstood lightning strikes and fires, a model of resistance and resilience. I've seen visitors stand nearby in a longing posture, as if wanting to imbibe its nature. It's a good thing that trees have such strong branches to bear the burden of our metaphors. As Michael Pollan writes, the meaning we ascribe to trees changes with history. What does that mean for our future together?

We people who stand on two legs could not be more different from the people who stand on their bole and roots. Autotroph versus heterotroph, sessile versus mobile, hot versus cold, collective versus individual identities—they are profoundly the "other" and yet they have a quality that calls us to emulate them. Strong as an oak, flexible as a willow, we ask them to teach us how to be more like them, how to transcend time, to grow, and to heal. Patiently they stand in the sun and show us.

I wonder if they grow weary of us projecting our meanings upon them, our aspirations to be like them. Strong as an oak, flexible as a willow. At least they don't reproach us when we fail. And how could we not? We are not trees. We lack their stillness, their presence, the generosity that comes from spinning sunlight to sugar. To stand in stillness for centuries requires ingenuity in harnessing physical forces and genius for collaboration. They learned long ago that the key to life as a sessile being is to cultivate good relationships, that all flourishing is mutual, especially when you can't run away. John Hay writes, "Trees stand deep within a kind of knowing that surpasses human knowledge."

The University of Wisconsin Arboretum was where the art and science of restoration was born, inspired in part by Aldo Leopold, who was its first research director. Its founders meant it to be a collection not of individuals but a living representation of all the ecological communities of Wisconsin. Here, trees are not posed as lonely objects; they are assembled according to their own shared predilections for certain soils and slant of afternoon light. A maple can't fully be a maple without trillium and wood thrush, and red oaks are not themselves without morels and blue jays. The notion of a new kind of arboretum was in response to Leopold's often repeated quote that "the first step to intelligent tinkering is to save all the pieces." And too many of the forest pieces are being lost.

These essays embody the idea that it is not enough to eulogize the nearly lost; we must try to bring them back: come read about torreya and hemlock and the people who protect their future. I'm reminded that the woods of the arboretum were developed on old cornfields and the footprint of an abandoned housing development. The land will teach us restoration, not only of trees themselves, but also of our relationship with them. We need not be passive consumers or companions of trees, treating them as a scaffold for our aspirations. We could view them as our relatives, as kinfolk we have treated badly and to whom we seek to make amends.

In this literary arboretum, we leave manicured grounds for the wildwoods, to revel in the golden haze of Rick Bass's charismatic larch, and to search out the largest being on the planet with Richard Preston's redwood encounter. Trees are not exemplars, metaphors, or scenery for our lives. We will live in a different world when we recognize the personhood of trees, who have their own rich cultural lives, absolutely without reference to our own. They have their own festivals of budding, fertility rites of pollen shed, autumnal extravagance, and winter dreaming, their own stories written in the cellulose pages of their own bodies.

These essays bring us into the presence of the most enduring beings on the planet. I think we would be a different kind of human had we permitted ourselves to live beneath big trees, in the shelter of our elders. But we are resistant to the teachings of humility, so resentful of their stature that we will not let them stand, save in our designated groves behind a velvet rope where we charge admission for awe. Humility is free.

Arboreta play a critical role in alleviating plant blindness, in helping to focus our attention on what truly sustains life on this forested planet. Neither my arboretum nor this literary one has a display for the most common relationship between people and trees. There is no section for clear-cutting or bulldozing or indentured servitude in plantations.

It is not lost on me that this book is written on the bodies of trees pulped, digested, pressed, polished, and printed to carry our stories into the world. Writers and readers alike owe a debt of gratitude—and more. These essays are acts of reciprocity, a down payment on the debt incurred.

As we give our attention to the old-growth forest and the beloved backyard shade tree, we recognize that paying attention to trees is only the beginning. Attention generates wonder, which generates more attention and more joy. Paying attention to the more-than-human world doesn't lead only to amazement; it leads also to acknowledgment of pain. Open and attentive, we see and feel equally the beauty and the wounds, the old growth and the clear-cut, the mountain and the mine. Paying attention to suffering sharpens our ability to respond. To be responsible. This, too, is a gift, for when we fall in love with the living world, we cannot be bystanders to its destruction. Attention becomes intention, which coalesces itself to action.

BALD CYPRESS

JULIA SHIPLEY

The Giving Tree

Part One: Fire

IN THE PREDAWN HOURS of Monday, January 16, 2012, Ed Forrest, an off-duty battalion chief for the Seminole County Fire Department, woke to a voice on his two-way radio. A request was out for Tanker 24 to respond to a fire in nearby Longwood. Forrest recalls lurching from his bed, confused: Longwood is a small city on the outskirts of Orlando; six-thousand-gallon water trucks like Tanker 24 are reserved for backcountry wildfires and infernos. Forrest called the dispatcher, who explained to him that the oldest tree in the state—a thirty-five-hundred-year-old bald cypress named The Senator—had burst into flames.

Within minutes Forrest was accelerating toward one of the last vestiges of primeval Florida, a towering organism that had been photosynthesizing sunlight a century before Moses and millennia before Socrates and Plato. A mile away Chief Forrest could see black smoke, and by the time he reached the forest preserve, streaking orange flames. Though the tree is normally hidden by lush vegetation, accessible only by a long narrow boardwalk, Forrest plainly saw the fireball engulfing The Senator's crown. The tree was, in firefighter terms, fully involved.

Forrest watched flames shoot out of the tree's full height, 118 feet above the ground. "It was like a blowtorch, or a Roman candle," he said. "It was heartbreaking to see."

It had been an exceptionally dry winter in Central Florida, and the fire had everything it needed—wood fuel, a good draft—to burn perfectly. A temperature-detecting camera estimated the heat at nearly a thousand degrees; fire chiefs considered sending a helicopter with a bandy bucket to dump lake water on the crown. Forrest craned his neck and watched embers spark into the sky. Already fully ablaze by the time crews arrived, it was too late: at eight a.m., the largest tree east of the Mississippi, one of the six eldest trees in the world, collapsed.

For a while, no one knew anything definitive about what caused the fire. All they knew was that overnight, the oldest living thing in Florida—a tree already three thousand years old when Ponce de León set foot on this peninsula in the early 1500s, a tree that had withstood innumerable lightning strikes, perhaps hundreds of hurricanes, and the logger's ax—had mysteriously ignited and was gone in a single morning. Beyond the plaque declaring the tree Florida's original spectacle, there was a huge hole in the sky.

A columnist for the *Orlando Sentinel* noted that a pile of twigs and branches had been discovered at the tree's base, and wondered whether someone had started this blaze deliberately. Had a homeless person let a campfire get out of control? Despite the otherwise calm evening, others suggested that lightning had struck the tree's exterior. A Division of Forestry investigator concluded: it burned from within.

The Florida that European explorers found in 1513 was columned in ancient bald cypresses, their soaring canopies hung with boughs of feathery foliage. Years later, the trees were prized by timber companies. Because cypress lumber does not rot, it became the most sought-after wood in the Southeast, used as cross ties for train tracks so that more trains could haul more logs out of the woods.

By the turn of the last century, Florida's 27 million acres of old-growth forest were almost completely felled. The biggest and best trees were taken first, and then the next best trees, and then all the trees. Today, two stands of virgin cypress remain: one in the Barley Barber Swamp in South Florida, the other in Corkscrew Swamp Sanctuary.

In the opening paragraphs of his self-published treatise, *Cypress: From Creation—Thru Exploitation—To Regeneration*, Marvin Buchanan, the operator of a wholesale nursery and the son, grandson, and great-grandson of lumbermen in Central Florida, writes, "During my short life of 60 years, I have seen very dramatic changes in the ecosystems in my small world of Lafayette County, Florida."

The way Buchanan sees it, man has sinned a long time against the land. The Creator made everything as it should be, he says, the right tree in the right place, and we've messed it up mightily. In his book, he tells of how virgin cypresses once had trunks more than fifteen feet wide. Buchanan's woodsman kin would first girdle the wood, and then return the following year to saw down the giant trees. Mule teams would drag carts, or, in some cases, pull boats, to bring the logs to mills. We took the best of the best, he says: trees, deer, turkey. Now, after generations of picking the good stuff, we're left with genetically inferior stock.

Given the rate at which Florida's forests were felled, The Senator's survival was an anomaly. By the early twentieth century, the tree was almost alone in an area of Florida whose logged acres became orange groves and artichoke farms and then suburbs in the shadow of Orlando. By the turn of the millennium, Big Tree Park, The Senator's eleven-acre home, was an island of green amid muffler shops and a wicker-chair factory; today it's bordered by General Hutchison Parkway and the Old Dixie Highway, in the vicinity of bail bondsmen and divorce attorneys, Big Lots and Starbucks, a fire station and the courthouse. The tree, at almost twelve stories, was taller than the Lincoln Memorial and towered above them all.

The Senator got its name from Florida senator Moses Overstreet, a man whose fortune was built from forest products, like turpentine and timber. And so it was ironic, perhaps, that Overstreet protected the behemoth tree from becoming railway ties or the frame of a now long-gone house. In the early 1900s he purchased it and its surrounding patch of wetland, and though Overstreet logged much of his parcel, he did not fell what was known back then as The Sentinel Tree—and thus forfeited its commercial potential. According to one newspaper, the tree contained the board feet to build five bungalows, or become a million boxes of toothpicks, with enough left over to cut into nine cords.

Though Overstreet might have considered cutting the tree, he was obviously dissuaded, and probably for reasons other than altruism. As some cypresses do, The Senator had a hollow on its far side large enough to crawl into. Its presence meant that the tree would never yield clean, full logs, which diminished the value of its lumber. By the mid-1920s Overstreet had become a Florida state senator, and when he donated his parcel of land to the town of Longwood, they renamed the tree in his honor.

Yet the great inner chamber, a detail that saved the tree from the lumber industry's saws, played a role in its demise.

According to police reports, in the dark hours before the fire department dispatcher awakened Ed Forrest, a twenty-six-year-old Floridian named Sara Barnes scrambled over the first fence surrounding Big Tree Park. She was with a friend, Thaddeus Peralta, who gave her a boost over the second fence, a wrought-iron one, surrounding The Senator itself. Once they crawled inside, the two stood within the shelter of the tree's great hollow, where the air was probably cool and pungent, the darkness almost absolute. Sara lit a small fire. The flame, she later said, was "for light," so she'd be able to take a hit of methamphetamine, paraphernalia for which was found in her possession.

Her fire accidentally kindled tinder in The Senator's dry interior, and the flames quickly blazed beyond her control. She and Thaddeus fled back over the fences. She considered trying to put out the fire, but it moved too swiftly. The pair drove to a nearby fast-food restaurant where they sat and watched fire trucks rush past.

Within days, Sara posted to her Facebook page a photo of flames engulfing the tree, followed by a comment: "I can't believe I burned down a tree older than Jesus." She was promptly arrested after and charged with unlawful burning of lands. When local news outlets ran the story, she became the subject of scathing criticism. She told police she was remorseful.

Part Two: Afterlives

Whereas The Senator has a thick file at the Museum of Seminole County History stuffed with a century's worth of newspaper clippings (which is accompanied by a hallway full of photos, artwork, and framed poems about the tree's existence), what we know about Sara Barnes fits a single page.

She has a bellybutton ring. She likes the Beatles. She sometimes plays poker online. She also plays guitar. She appreciates marijuana. Growing up, her family had a Chihuahua named Sophie.

According to her autobiographical profile on Model Mayhem, a website for professional models: "I am a diamond waiting to shine for the world in ways beauty and intelligence can only be used to describe. I am a nature enthusiast and I love capturing nature at its best, which is always, through a camera."

It's likely that Sara's relationship with The Senator began long before the morning of January 16, 2012, maybe when she was a little girl. Her first visit to the tree might have been with a parent, a tradition among many Florida families, during which mothers and fathers share with their children the giant cypress they glimpsed as kids. Or perhaps she arrived via an elementary school field trip, clambering off the bus, led by teachers, to trek the boardwalk to the home of the impossibly tall tree. She would have squinted, her head tipped to its limit to distinguish the tree's branches and foliage far off in the sky.

Later, as an adolescent, she might have visited the tree after dark, as part of an illicit rite of passage. (Teenagers were rumored to sneak into the concealed hollow late at night.) Maybe Sara continued coming to the tree even as she entered her twenties, for a reprieve from Florida's punishing heat. In addition to providing shade from its canopy, the cypress tends to pool cool air in its hollows, furnishing a tiny breeze. As the pressures of adulthood mounted, maybe The Senator seemed like a sanctuary.

Certainly that's the feeling that Sam, the boy at the heart of the young adult classic *My Side of the Mountain,* has when he encounters a big tree in a northeastern forest. Readers of that book open to the first page and encounter Sam holed up in a snowstorm, snuggled within the cavity of a hemlock six feet in diameter. Though the outside air is bitter cold, "I can sit here inside my tree," he attests, "and write with bare hands." Sam builds a little fire for warmth, aided by "a chimney that leads the smoke out through a knothole."

My Side of the Mountain was initially refused for publication on the grounds that it could induce youth to quit their bedrooms and make for the woods, where they might each find a hollowed-out tree for shelter. Nevertheless, Jean Craighead George's book was printed in 1959, and now, more than fifty years later, it's a staple of young people's literature.

Maybe Sara Barnes was once one of those readers. Let's say you grew up a thousand miles south of Sam's hemlock in the Catskills, where, instead of rustling leaves, you heard the sound of wind in palms—the impulse to hole up in some great benevolence would appeal to you just the same, yes? Perhaps some half-remembered version of this was what Sara had in mind when she slipped inside the hollow of the thirty-five-hundred-year-old bald cypress while most of greater Orlando was still asleep.

"Standing before the biggest and the oldest and the most king-like of them all, I suddenly had an idea," Sam tells us in *My Side of the Mountain.* "Inside I felt as cozy as a turtle in its shell."

It's worth considering—just for a moment—that there might be more to Sara than what the police reports and scornful newspaper articles suggest. And it's worth noting that, at the end of February 2014, after being pulled over under suspicion of drunk driving, a police report detailed how she began to weep, saying that she didn't want to go to jail, that she'd already served time for burning the tree. That she loved trees.

Once, two years after The Senator was burned, I spoke to Sara briefly over the phone. I shared my hunch that the tree had been significant to her, and not just on that fateful night. She agreed, confirming that she had visited it throughout her life. I asked if there was a reason she went there to take drugs as opposed to any other place. Had she read *My Side of the Mountain*? Was she trying to follow Sam's retreat, and take shelter inside the hollow of a being she'd known since childhood?

"No," she replied. "But do you know *The Giving Tree*?"

The Giving Tree, an illustrated children's book by Shel Silverstein, is another young adult classic. It describes a tree's life-giving service to a human who, as a toddler, gazes up into its canopy and swings beneath its limbs, and then later, as a growing boy, climbs up into its branches, happily chomping its fruit. Time passes, and the boy is a teenager carving letters into the tree's trunk. He returns as an adult to cut and sell the tree for lumber. The tree and the human are united once more when, well into old age, the man comes to sit on his childhood tree's stump and rest.

"That's one of my favorite books," Sara said, "and that's how I look at what happened. Basically the tree saved my life. I didn't intentionally burn it down. I was addicted to meth for eight years, and now I've been sober for two. But, like I said, I owe my life,

I am alive, because of that tree."

What Sara meant by this is unclear. Was the fiery end of The Senator the beginning of her adult sobriety? Can killing a tree save a person? We can't know: following a probation violation of her original suspended sentence, Sara served two and a half years in prison for possession of methamphetamine and drug paraphernalia and unlawful burning of lands. She no longer speaks about the incident.

The Senator always drew a crowd. Long before Spanish sailors reached the New World, the Miccosukee and Seminole Indians used the towering cypress as a landmark, a guidepost for finding their way on their annual migration inland from the coast. Centuries later, in 1931, a photograph of The Senator shows members of the Christian Fellowship gathered beneath the canopy. Eleven people stand shoulder to shoulder, equating the tree's girth. Another photo, taken in 1928, shows two men standing spread eagle across the trunk. Like God reaching for Adam and Adam reaching back, you can see their fingers just barely touch, and where they touch, you can see inscriptions carved in the bark: LMB, MC, CMB.

In the late 1800s, an entrepreneur named Mr. Lord hitched his work mule to a cart to haul the curious over for a look-see at the magnificent tree. Back then, visitors got off the cart and hopped from log to log. Later, in the first decades of the 1900s, they traversed a boardwalk of palmetto stumps. By 1929 there were concession stands, souvenir postcards, and a presidential dedication; soon there was an official plaque, lightning rods, and an increment borer to obtain a core sample. In the endless parade to see The Senator were daisy chains of generations, kids who grew into parents who grew into grandparents and great-grandparents, the elders taking the young by the hand to meet the tree. Through it all, people tried—unsuccessfully—to propagate genuine Senator offspring, so that these visits could continue in perpetuity.

"No one has yet been able to collect [The Senator's] cones that produce seeds," a reporter wrote in the *Orlando Sentinel* in 1991. The scant cones they did find were duds. In 1999, one man was dispatched to climb up and take clippings for the Florida Champion Tree Project; however, the lab handling the clones—an outfit with patented techniques and a contract to grow forests for Disneyland—struck out.

But one day, in 1997, in a series of events unknown at the time to reporters and park administrators, a man named Laymond Hardy drove up from Miami, parked in the lot of Big Tree Park, and proceeded to do something remarkable.

Hardy, who passed away in 2013, was a high school science teacher, but he had also been recognized as a horticulturalist, a genetics researcher, and an accomplished naturalist. One friend declared him "a one-man consulting firm in a variety of biological subject matter." He bred a Columbian orchid to a Georgian orchid to develop a cold-tolerant orchid called the Enduracold. He invented the inverted root graft, a technique for establishing commercial plantings of pond apples and oranges. He helped the Bahamas establish kiwi fruits.

A photograph of Hardy shows a stocky man with a mostly kempt shock of sandy hair, his slightly cherubic face burdened with thick glasses. There's one of him playing harmonica. There's another where he tends his honeybees, shirtless.

During his visit to Big Tree Park in 1997, Hardy might have spent the day gawking at The Senator or prowling the nearby hammock swamp. But what's certain is that winds from a recent storm had sheared off a limb of the famous cypress, which Hardy picked up and used to swat mosquitoes. After squishing around, studying dragonflies and cabbage palms, he returned to his car and stuck the branch in the seat beside him. Leaving Big Tree Park, he steered the car northwest toward the town of Mayo, almost two hundred miles away, where Marvin Buchanan, the aforementioned great-grandson of lumbermen and the author of *Cypress*, lives.

In the late 1980s, in an effort to preserve native cypress, Buchanan began collecting seeds from the purest stands of pond cypress along the banks of the Suwannee River. He used the seeds to propagate an orchard of superior genetics, and with the help of a genetic researcher at the University of Florida School of Forestry, he adopted clone technology. When Hardy handed over his switch from The Senator, Buchanan used the buds on the branch to begin ten clones of the famous tree.

In August 2013, Seminole County's board of commissioners called Buchanan to purchase two of the seven surviving clones, which are now eighteen years old. They were transported by truck and installed just over a year after The Senator's destruction. The one planted in Big Tree Park, near where the charred remnants of its three-and-a-half-millennia-old parent still stands, is young and feathery but biding its time. It's called The Phoenix.

Ursula K. Le Guin

Kinship

Very slowly burning, the big forest tree
stands in the slight hollow of the snow
melted around it by the mild, long
heat of its being and its will to be
root, trunk, branch, leaf, and know
earth dark, sun light, wind touch, bird song.

Rootless and restless and warmblooded, we
blaze in the flare that blinds us to that slow,
tall, fraternal fire of life as strong
now as in the seedling two centuries ago.

TAIWAN CEDAR

JESSICA J. LEE

The Coffin Trees

WINTER RAIN in Taiwan's mountains seems to hang in the air, getting into every seam of my clothes. The weather was warm when I left the city, but two thousand meters up, in the cloud forests near Alishan, I am shaking with cold.

I was told the trail would be fairly easy. A worthwhile distraction from my grief over my grandfather's death. I'd spent the autumn tracing his past in Taiwan, restlessly trying to close the gap left by my family's migration to Canada and my own moves throughout Europe. In hiking, I found a way of connecting not just with my family's culture but also with the land they loved.

The trail rises gently for the first few hours. A narrow track traces a ridge past a disused logging road, then enters swaths of silver grass so high it brushes against my lips. It is a day of muted color, the green and gray of dull coins and steamed-up windows. It hasn't been difficult, but the rain has left me exhausted, sensitive to every movement of my body.

Reaching the cypress forest, where soil springs back underfoot, I feel somehow energized again. The trees plunge me from the immediacy of walking into a much longer timescale. I scan the periphery for cypresses the girth of a car or a house, something slower and bigger that I can focus my mind on. Sound is muffled by the fog that hugs the ancient trees. I cannot hear my footsteps.

But the moment I lose myself in the calm of the forest, I am forced back to attention: forty minutes of scrambling down a wet slope toward the lake. When I finally reach the shore and the trees I've come to see, the sun has dipped low in the evening sky. My own sense of time and scale has been rattled entirely.

In 1999, a 7.3 magnitude earthquake reeled across Taiwan, toppling buildings and killing thousands across much of the center and north of the country. It was the strongest earthquake in sixty-four years, hurling landslides on mountain towns, exposing subsoil once deep underground along fault lines. In the foothills of the Central Mountains, one of these landslides blocked a river. And it was here that the 水漾森林 (Shuiyang Senlin) was created: an earthquake-dammed lake in the middle of an old-growth cedar forest.

The forest is predominantly cedar and false cypress, and the logging roads were cut in the early half of the twentieth century as Japanese colonial forestry served to source trees for temple building, furniture, oils, and medicines, and to map the land, thus effectively colonizing it. One of the species, *Taiwania cryptomerioides,* is known in English as the "coffin tree" for its use in coffins.

In 1906, a young Japanese botanist named Bunzō Hayata published the cedar's name after examining a sample taken from the slopes of Yushan in Taiwan's Central Mountain Range.

With drooping, scaly fronds, the tree looked quite similar to the enormous false cypresses that grew nearby. But on closer inspection—particularly of its seed cones—Hayata found it more closely resembled the Japanese *Cryptomeria* (meaning "hidden parts"). Hayata—keen to establish Taiwanese flora on the world stage—named the species *Taiwania* for the island, *cryptomerioides* for its resemblance to his own native cedar.

But the coffin trees were not, in fact, endemic to Taiwan, nor were Hayata's the first samples collected. Specimens had been gathered in Yunnan, China, and northern Myanmar, and since Hayata's naming of the species, small populations of *Taiwania* have likewise been identified in Vietnam.

In every place the cedars have been found, a demand for its timber has followed. In the early decades of the twentieth century, the English botanist Frank Kingdon-Ward wrote of timber yards set up deep in Chinese forests, cutting planks from the trees directly where they were felled. By the 1950s, Taiwanese foresters were forced to take inventory of what few old-growth cedars remained.

Taiwania is a tree that remains rare today—the International Union for Conservation of Nature (IUCN) lists it as vulnerable. Where it has been planted as an ornamental, it fails to reach the maturity it has known in the wild, growing lanky and distorted instead. But once, this tree thrived. Fossil records of it have been found as far away as Alaska, from 100 million years ago, and Europe, some 60 million years ago, across the continents my family now calls home.

The coffin trees, left to their own devices, live unimaginably long lives—up to two thousand years. This longevity is matched by height. In the Indigenous Rukai language, they are known as "trees that reach the moon." And so it is that the cedars stretch time, growing higher than every other tree in the canopy, two hundred feet toward the sky. No seedlings crowd the forest floor. To survive, the *Taiwania* waits, instead, for disturbance.

In the years since the earthquake flooded this forest, the cedars have grown bare, and their needled crowns have disintegrated. The tree trunks now stand literally dead in the water: bleached in the sunlight, bared of their bark. As years pass, water level recedes, and soon, I am told, the lake won't be here at all.

But where the coffin trees once grew, new life is emerging: at the break between wood and water, moss and grasses grow, frilling the old tree trunks with green. Silver fish dart in the shallows, and freshwater crabs and shrimp dance in the sediment.

What might grow here years from now, I cannot say. It is busy with hikers like me, setting camp on the lake's shore. The old trees are decayed and fall every so often, so we take care to set our tents far from the standing wood.

I cannot count how many years have brought the cedars to this moment. The sun sets behind the distant hills, and the once-forest and its lake are cast in shadow. At this border between old and new growth, I sleep.

ANDREA COHEN

First Thought,
Best Thought

I'm three or four,
hidden in the branches

of the cherry tree.
I don't ask: how

did I get here?
I don't fear falling.

The job of the blossom
is to bloom, to be

beautifully unschooled in ruin.

OSAGE ORANGE

WILLIAM BRYANT LOGAN

The Things Trees Know

A look inside their secret lives

T O STUDY HOW TREES GROW is to admire not only their persistence but also their imagination. Live wood just won't quit. Every time you knock it down, it comes back again, but when a plant sprouts back, it is not a random shot, like some finger simply raised to make a point. Rather, the growing tip of any stem—what botanists call the meristem— answers with an inborn, complex pattern, like a musical tune. Something had knocked the top off a London plane tree in Brooklyn. It had already been forty feet tall. It hadn't just sprouted a new arrow-upright stem. The sprouts at the broken edge had ramified into a set of eight complete little plane trees, each one closely resembling what its parent had looked like twenty years before, a bouquet atop the trunk.

In a grove of ancient junipers beside a village in the Spanish province of Castile, one trunk had cracked and bent until it ran horizontal, parallel to the ground. All along the trunk had sprung a linear grove of new young junipers, each with the same ancestral shape.

A little branch had broken off a willow and fallen into a stream. Where it had fetched up at an eddying edge farther downstream, it had rooted, sprouted, and up had come a new tree, whose structure had been just like its parent's.

Charlie Parker is supposed to have given the following advice to a young saxophone player. First, you had to learn your instrument. Next, you had to learn to play the tunes. Finally, you were free to improvise, to play jazz. John Coltrane's "My Favorite Things" is a terrific example of what he meant. It begins with a perfectly clean statement of the tune, beautiful in itself for the richness of its tone, notes that are almost solid, so you could build a house out of them. Within three minutes, the tune has modulated into completely unexpected shapes, sizes, rising and falling glissades, stops and starts, pianissimos to fortes, but it never loses the thread of that original tune. Every tree is a jazz player, in just this way, although where a long Coltrane piece might last a quarter hour, a tree's performance may go on for half a millennium or more.

The tropical botanists Francis Hallé and Roelof Oldeman were the first to articulate the idea that every plant first grows to fill a form—that is, to play its tune. It does not matter whether it is a weed by the wall or a giant sequoia, whether it is a tropical *Terminalia* or a subarctic birch. They, along with P. B. Tomlinson in their 1978 book *Tropical Trees and Forests*, wrote that every species of the higher plants can grow in only one of twenty-three different patterns. (They have since added one more.) In fact, they noticed, a few modulate from one pattern to another, and a few more seem to grow in a hybrid pattern, but all conform to the same morphology that their ancestors had.

The tree's "chops" are inborn, a part of its inheritance. It knows how to grow in the way its parents did. The seed contains the knowledge. To learn its "charts," the plant grows to elaborate this knowledge into its basic shape. This first statement of its tune may take a few weeks for the weed or twenty years for the oak or may last a lifetime for a fir, but in physiological time, it is just the same. All seek to fill out the pattern of stem, lateral, flower, and fruit that was handed down to it by its forebears.

What are its notes, its scales, its sharps, its flats, and its time signatures? According to the three botanists, every plant plays upon six choices:

The First—To branch or not to branch. Palms, for example, never branch, though some clustering palms make the second choice, as follows.

The Second—If you branch, do you do so only at the bottom, or all along a stem? Bamboo, for example, is simply a colony of stems, each repeating from the base, and the small grove is in fact a single plant. Quaking aspen seems the same, but each of its new sprouts itself branches all up and down the stem. Shrubs, likewise, in general prefer the mode of living that sprouts again and again from the base.

The Third—Do your trunk and branches grow without a rest, or is there a dormant season? Most trees in the temperate zone choose the latter gambit. Trees with a definite dormant season—like spruce and fir—tend to have a very clean and open habit of growth.

The Fourth—Do all of your branches want to grow upward, all outward, or do some want to grow upward and others outward? Pagoda dogwood prefers to grow mainly outward. Staghorn sumac wants to grow mainly upward. On upward-growing, or orthotropic, stems, the leaves and twigs tend to be organized symmetrically around the stem, in spirals of opposite pairs. On outward-growing, or plagiotropic, branches, leaves and twigs appear in flattened planes along the edges of the branch, like a phalanx of wings.

The Fifth—Do you flower at the branch tips, or on smaller lateral branches? Again, sumac flowers at the terminals, so each year's new growth must start from dormant laterals below the tips. It makes what look like bucks' horns, hence the common name "staghorn sumac." (In one species, the sprouts even have the velvet of young horns.) If you flower on laterals—like most temperate-zone trees, such as maples and ash—you can continue to grow more or less straight upward while your branches go straight outward, and if any difficulties occur, one growing tip can substitute for another.

The Sixth—Do your branches change back and forth between growing outward and growing upward? This is a flexible arrangement that lets a plant fill the space above and around it. Frequent changes of upward-growing top branches allow it to exploit more sun to one side or the other. Hemlock is one example. It is wonderful to see how, for all of its ability to reach eighty and more feet in height, it has a nodding top that easily trades off its leading upright branch. On average, the leader changes seven times in ten years. The top of a hemlock is a juggler.

Out of these six choices, each plant plays its tune, the phrase that has characterized its kind for millions of years. No matter where its seed sprouts, each will try to play its melody. Many of the twenty-three-plus possible tunes are played only in the tropics, where abundant water and little cold let plant imaginations run wild. In the temperate zone, where winter is winter and where inundation may be followed by drought, fewer and more flexible tunes are the rule. The three botanists named all of the models in honor of other botanists who had studied the trees that exemplify that form. Rauh's model is the most common among temperate trees. Here, the trunk and branches are functionally equivalent, so if necessary one can become the other. It flowers on lateral branches, not tips, so it does not need to bifurcate to go on growing. It rests in winter and leafs again in spring. Troll's model is the next most common. Here again, the flowers are lateral, and the plants take a rest in dormancy. The plants are never merely a single trunk or assembly of trunks. Their branches waffle: when they begin life, they want to grow out, not up, but at the end of the season their tips turn upward. Here is a tune with a phrase that stretches out all year, only to run up the scale at the end, but again, as in Rauh, the effect is to let the plant expand both out and up. A third common model in the temperate zone is Massart's, although it is a relic of an older world. Spruces, firs, and many of the conifers play this tune. Their trunks are upright, but their branches only want to grow outward. Because they rest in winter, they tend to have a very neat and consistent growth habit, both upward and outward. They grow both up and out in what look like whorls.

When conifers ruled the world, in the warm and equable time before the ice, they had little need of improvisation. Massart's conical model is well adapted to capturing light, and it holds its neighbor at arm's length. Even on mountaintops at tree line, the balsam fir simply loses its tops to the wind, but its long-reaching plagiotropic branches spread out in a carpet over the ground.

Leafy trees never had it that good. They began to spread through the evolving continents as the weather started turning nastier, around 150 million years ago. Not only that, but the damn conifers had already taken over almost every place worth living. The flowering plants, dominant today, were then marginal, sneaky, eking out a living along streamsides, on rock ledges, anyplace where light could get in and where a conifer couldn't make it. From the beginning, they specialized in not specializing. Not only did they not grow in such a regular shape, they also took whatever shape they had made and reiterated it throughout their lives. Perversely, the leafy trees often started with competing branches, letting them fight it out on their way to sky, so that if one perished, another might make its way higher and wider.

Most of us, even those of us who take care of trees, have a vague notion that there are different ways of growing. Yes, an oak or an ash or a maple look qualitatively different from a catalpa or an ailanthus or a horse chestnut, from a honey locust, a beech, or an elm. But just how we can seldom say anymore, though our ancestors almost certainly could have told us quite certainly what the difference was. They lived constantly among the trees, and their lives depended upon how those trees grew.

Still, a few species stand out. Staghorn sumac races along the edge of difficult disturbed sites much as the first leafy plants must have done during the early and middle Cretaceous period. It loves the loaf-shaped substrate upon which superhighways perch. Spreading clonally—that is, by means of an aggressive underground root system—it occupies more and more exposed soil of the raised berms. Often, it is in a race with quaking aspen, another clonal spreader. There is a spot near Oneonta, New York, on Interstate 88, where the two spread so quickly, you can almost see them charging into each other like linemen trying to open a hole for the back. Who gets there first tends to get to stay there, and the slopes are a great place to catch the light they need to grow.

The pair are like Laurel and Hardy. Each aspen is straight, skinny, and gray. They stand close together like a roomful of partygoers. Each sumac is beyond paunchy. It is downright fat and squat. A flower blooms always at the end of a new stem, so that end will never grow again. Two lateral buds beneath the flower sprout instead, and they grow out in wide open arcs like two hands raised to signal a touchdown. The following year, those two branches flower, so the same thing happens all over again. The plants less climb into the sky than they reach out to capture as much aerial real estate as they can. Two by two by two by two, each trunk ramifies into an impossibly complicated candelabra.

Most of the models make ways to mix the tall and the broad. Many of the trees in the temperate forest—the oak, the ash, the maple, the pine—grow straight up with lateral branches that also arch upward. All have spiral or opposite twigs, leaves, and flowers. The form is marvelously supple. If the top stem fails, the next lateral down turns upward to take over the leader position. Any branch can take the place of any other. If you are looking for opportunity in the dense forest, this is a fine model to follow.

Trees of equal or even greater size—the elms, the beech, the honey locust—instead grow only spreading branches. They get taller only because one new sideways branch sprouts atop the previous one, and so on sometimes to heights of more than a hundred feet. They get a little additional upward boost because in the dormant season of their first year, the new floppy branch may slightly straighten up. A quarter of all temperate-forest trees grow this way. It is even more flexible than the upright model, because the sideways branches can stretch in any direction to find light, staying short if light is scarce or stretching out forty feet to reach a hole in the forest canopy. So a tree of this kind can go upward or outward as conditions change. These are the trees that make great vase-shaped canopies, so that a double row of elms or even of honey locusts above a roadway shuts out the sky above.

Still others play a tune that sends up each year a trio or more of fresh stems, all fighting one another for the light. Ailanthus trees do this, as do catalpas and horse chestnuts. Of the three or more fresh upright stems, one dominates and the others bend off sideways. As these are often lovely flowering trees, at the right time of year the trees look like a fireworks display, with explosions of leaf and flowers at each elevation, measuring back to when the tree was small. They seem to thrive on complication.

If every tree seeks to express its model, why then does the world of plants not resemble immense phalanxes of similar shapes? Why is a forest not an array like the bottles of different brands of seltzer on the supermarket shelf?

Because of the many accidents.

Because of the uncertain world.

Because of heat and cold, storm and wind, pests and diseases

Because of neighbors, those that are rooted, and others that are two-, four-, six-, and eight-legged.

Because of opportune openings to the sun.

Because of the subsequent improvisation.

Reiteration is the wonderful name that Oldeman gave the tree's ability to respond to the world around it by in whole or in part replaying its melody, but in very different contexts at ever different scales. It is jazz: take the tune, stretch it, cut it into pieces, put them back together, transpose it up or down, flatten it out, or shoot it at the sky. Each tree gets its chops, gets its charts, and then throws them away. It knows the chart by heart, and so can repeat it with a thousand variations for hundreds of years, as it grows to its full stature, lives among its peers, and grows back down to the ground. Positive and negative morphogenesis, they dubbed the cycle: growing up and growing down.

As soon as the tune is played, the initial reiteration is the first major branch. As a leafy tree grows, it will generate what arborists call scaffold branches. These are the few—maybe five to eight— very large stems upon which the tree will hang most of its crown— that is, most of its smaller branches and their millions of leaves. As horticulturalist Liberty Hyde Bailey saw as far back as 1908, "A tree is essentially a collection of a colony of individual parts. . . . Branches are not so much organs as competing individuals." The skill of the tree as an organism is like Coltrane in his vamping: it brings the variations back to the persisting theme.

Atop these scaffold branches—big, thick, and arching—come a series of smaller reiterated steps at the scale of trees, as though they were dogwoods or cherries, filling up what will be the middle story of the mature tree. Next are reiterations at the scale of a shrub, bushing out the leafy twigs to all sides where life-giving sun is to be found. Finally, when the tree is about to achieve its full size, the repetitions are practically the size of herbaceous plants. Each new sprout complex extends only a foot or two from the parent branch.

All the new branchlets will remain forever small in diameter. The tropical botanists call this last layer the Monkeys' Lawn.

The first third of the tree's life is positive morphogenesis. "Building up" is what it means. The phase may last a hundred years. Then, for another century or two, the tree may maintain its full stature, no longer able to grow much taller or wider but still replacing every lost piece of the Monkeys' Lawn or the shrub layer with fresh improvisations. Finally, it enters on the third stage of its life, negative morphogenesis, or "growing down." An old saying about oak trees put it succinctly: "Three hundred years growing, three hundred years living, three hundred years dying."

Growing down is not just decay. It is as active and improvisational as was the building up. Roots are damaged or die. Branches are lost to storms. Hollows open up on the trunk and are colonized by fungi like the wonderful and aptly named dryad's saddle. The tree's solid circulation system resolves itself back into discrete pathways, some living and some dead. It becomes obvious that scaffold branches were once separate trees, as they become so again, some maintaining their root systems and others losing them. Now the tips of the higher branches begin to die back. Instead of growing new reiteration branchlets on their undersides, as they did in their youth, they now sprout perfect little trees of their species on the tops of the branches, between the trunk and the dead tips. It is a complete restatement of the thematic tune, happening dozens of times among the still-living branches.

Now that we know trees can spend a third of their lives in this process, arborists are no longer so eager to remove a tree once symptoms of age set in. By studying and keeping up with the plant's own process of growing down, the pruner can keep the tree safe and lovely for many years longer than was once thought possible. People have determinate life spans. Trees do not. Although the trunk and branches are old and decaying, the creature is still producing the brand-new babies of the reiterated stems. An ancient tree is thus a mixture of newborns and Methuselah. By helping it to retrench, we can keep it for longer.

Little by little, a tree loses its crown, first small branches, then larger ones. Roots decay. The circulation system that carries water aloft to the leaves starts to break down. When no leaves emerge on a branch, it can no longer feed itself. It dies and falls to the ground, but the tree does not give up. When a giant that was once ninety feet tall has shrunk to a height of twenty feet, little images of itself may sprout from the lower trunk or even from the root flare, wherever a living connection between root and branch survives. I once saw an ash on the Somerset Levels that had left just a single sprout on the trunk and one from just above the roots. All the rest of the trunk was dead and its base stood in a posture that looked like a dancer's plié. It is not impossible that one or the other of those last sprouts—if only they can generate their own stable root systems— may grow once again to ninety feet tall. Phoenix regeneration is the name for this process. Potentially, every tree is immortal.

The fine British arborist Neville Fay outlined the seven ways that this regeneration can happen: One of the reiterations at the base of the trunk can make its own root system and its own new trunk, as the ash I saw on the Levels was doing. An old scaffold branch can do the same. Or the tree may completely resprout from the basal root system, rising again from the ground up. Or the tree's lowest branches may strike the ground, root where they hit, and generate a new tree. Or a small-diameter trunk can form right inside the decaying ancient one and there make a fresh start. Or new roots may start in the hollow at the base of the tree, and touching ground, they may generate a new trunk and crown. Finally, the tree may fall right over, its lateral branches turning into new trees.

I had clients on the eastern shore of Maryland. Their house was bowered in a forest garden. They owned hundred-foot oaks, huge pecans, beautiful Chinese chestnuts, mature southern magnolias, a unique double allée of gigantic deodar cedars, but the very best of their trees was a fallen Osage orange. By most accounts, it is not a high-value species. Michael Dirr, whose *Manual of Woody Landscape Plants* is the standard reference for park and garden trees, commented, "Not worth recommending for the residential landscape." It drops fruit like corrugated puke green cannonballs, and the wood is so hard that to hand-saw through a dead trunk can wear out two grown men. Indeed, my clients showed the tree to me sheepishly. We rounded a corner of their house, admiring a huge pin oak in the distance, and there in the foreground was the fallen tree.

I stopped, and I believe my mouth must have fallen open.

"What do you think of it?" asked the wife, wrinkling her brow. I could see she was mentally gritting her teeth against what I was about to say.

"Amazing!" I replied.

Their brows both unfurrowed. A smile broadened on her face, but she wanted to make sure.

"You like it?" she asked.

"It is extraordinary," I answered. "The best of all your trees."

"Oh, what a relief," she breathed. "We were told we should remove it."

I expressed shocked disbelief. I think I may have thrown up my hands and pretended to tear my hair.

There on the ground before us was a trunk about forty feet long and about three feet in girth. It had fallen over so many years ago that ferns, mosses, and small herbaceous plants had colonized the root plate that stood at one end taller than a tall man. Because it was an Osage orange, however—renowned for its resistance to decay—the entire length of the trunk was otherwise intact. At the opposite end was the wonder.

Once they had been branches on the trunk, but when the tree had fallen, the former branches had changed their minds. The original crown of the tree had died away. All the other branches had died, but these two had risen straight into the air, as though they were and had the perfect right to be new young Osage orange trees. Decades later, each of them was forty feet tall. One was evidently still depending upon the remaining roots in the ground on the bottom of the root plate. The other had also begun to put down its own root system, snaking over the dead trunk and into the ground.

It is as though a person rested her arm on the dirt, spread out her palm, and two perfect new arms emerged from her lifeline, complete with all the muscles and tendons and circulation, the hands, palms, fingers, and fingernails. Or perhaps more accurate, as though a person lay down at night and had two new people over-night sprout from his torso, complete from toenails to cowlicks. I think John Coltrane would have loved phoenix regeneration. It is like those moments in "My Favorite Things" where the whole piece seems about to jump off the top end of the soprano sax register, but suddenly the tune takes up again.

We think we know a tree when we can name its genus and species, perhaps place it in a family, and recount the tale of invisible processes like photosynthesis and the production of pigments. What if this were really a strange, abstract, and less useful way of knowing trees than to know them by the forms in which they grow, live, and die? Up until the Neolithic and probably even into the Middle Ages, human beings were better at the latter than the former way. In those times too, they had a very active relationship to trees, depending on them for energy, warmth, structure. (Nowadays, we think we have graduated to oil, but that is only a way of robbing the energy of ancient trees.) In those days, we knew trees the way we know friends: what they like and don't like, how they are likely to respond to a thing we do with them, what we should under no circumstances try with them. Each exchanged with the other. There is no call to think people had to be altruists to do this. Rather, they knew what was good for them better than we do.

DORIANNE LAUX

Roots

The pine clings to the cliff side, angles
seaward above the waves, its exposed roots
attended by flowering weeds. Those fingers

will someday lose their grip. This is clear
to any one of us. And I believe the tree, too,
knows its long life will be cut short and

doesn't care. Why would it? Who among us
wouldn't give a year or more to lean against
the wind and gaze down into the void? And

doesn't this dark desire to fall exist in every heart?
I remember my first fast car ride at midnight,
stoplights streaking by, rings of fire on that beach

where I first dipped my tongue into the wet
salty cave of the beloved's mouth, the fury
with which I took the other's flesh inside me,

the hard pits of the first fruit I chewed and sucked.
Now, in my calm backyard, I watch clouds
tear themselves apart around the stars,

listen to the possum's claws rake and rasp
against the trashcan's metal sides, inhale
the blossoming cherry growing up over

the shed's flat roof. She drops her petals there
to make a carpet of snow. Even this far from
the ocean she knows what is possible, yet

is content to stand here, burrowing
into the clay earth, feeder roots worming
through hair-thin holes in the rusted

underground pipes. Even so, her lithe arms
sway in the night breeze and a few
of her bright petals settle onto the black pond.

They float only a moment before the moon-
colored carp finds them with his hairy ancient lips,
and one by one, carries them down.

SUGAR MAPLE

ROBIN MACARTHUR

Sugaring

ALF THE PEOPLE on your road park their cars near the highway and walk; the other half fasten their seat belts, take a deep breath, and gun it, bucking ruts and jerking wheels as their bodies get slammed this way and that. The kids on the school bus hold on to the seats in front of them and scream as the bus driver (your mother) presses the pedal to the floor, tightens her jaw, and keeps the bus pointed forward with bedrock determination. Car struts get shot, the alignment goes out of whack. You step out of your car in the driveway and your boots sink down six inches. You track it onto the porch, and into the hall, and into the kitchen. Ten miles away, in the town with paved streets, people are wearing sundresses and sandals; you're still in jeans and the Muck Boots you've been wearing for six months straight. Around here, March and April are called "mud season."

But there is one consolation. Mud season is also sugaring season. They go hand in hand during these cold nights, warm days. The frost under the roads settles, creating sinkholes; the sap in

the maple trees runs, filling buckets. You walk down the road with
your two-year-old daughter to the sugarhouse, looking, hoping, for
steam, and there it is: a thick waft of sweet, moist air billowing out
of the vented roof. Inside, your parents are throwing logs into the
evaporator, checking levels, pouring beautiful resin-colored syrup
into the glass Mason jars neighbors have brought by. Firelight
shimmers through the cracks of the iron doors. You run across the
(muddy) road with your daughter to collect sap and watch her press
her lips against the metal spigot; from where you stand it looks like
she is kissing the tree.

"Yum!" she exclaims, pulling away, her face smeared with sap
and tree bark and moss and snot.

People drop by: a family bearing bowls of soup, a single man
proffering a six-pack of beer. It's an open house, the sugar shack,
and everyone knows it. This dropping in is a way of keeping the
sugar makers company—they're in here for ten hours at a time
most days—but it's also what happens to people in spring. You
begin to thaw. You want to see faces again, converse, be outside for
long stretches of time. Neighbors bring in wood; you scoop scum
from the back pans; your daughter pulls out empty plastic jugs for
your mother to fill. The fire hisses. The steam rises. You crack open
beers. A party: "Sugar Boogie," your dad and daughter call it.

That night you make pizzas, cooking them on the open grate
of the evaporator door. You throw on red pepper, fresh mozzarella,
pesto from last summer's garden. You sit on old tractor and bus
seats turned into makeshift chairs and eat off your hands. Later
someone steps through the door with a bottle of Glenlivet and cups.
Last year you all determined, after much sampling, the perfect
combination of Scotch and near-syrup; now you attempt to find

that perfect ratio once more. Outside it grows dark. The room fills with hooting laughter. Once in a while you hear a car revving up the road, gunning it through deep pockets of mud. You watch the steam, the fire, the glistening faces, and you're glad you're not in that car, out on those roads, trying to get somewhere.

You step out the back door to take a leak in the snow and look up—sparks shooting out of the rusted chimney, an ash-flecked moon rising above the trees. You could go back inside, but instead you linger for a while: pants down, grinning, grateful for this dissolution of walls and of boundaries between inside and out, for this synchronicity between what the trees do and what people do, for the fact that it's (finally) warm enough for you to be out here half-naked, knee deep in a pile of snow, not wanting to be anywhere but the very spot your boots are planted.

HEMLOCK

ROBERT SULLIVAN

Forest Farewell

An ode to an iconic tree

WE HAVE GATHERED together today in a still-dark grove on the side of a hill to hear a few words about hemlock. We are a small group and there are not many words. Nothing anyone can say possibly sums up the long life of hemlock on the eastern seaboard of North America, which began about 30 million years ago and includes a long stretch of time that runs from the early Pleistocene era, as glaciers came and went, up until the arrival from East Asia of a tiny sapsucking bug, the hemlock woolly adelgid, which landed in the United States around the time Calvin Coolidge made it into office.

Thanks to the woolly adelgid's slow move north with warmer weather, the hemlock is dead or dying, half of its vast range disintegrated, the most northern extent on its way out. In just a few years, the forest we are standing in today will no longer be standing. A eulogy is maybe a little ahead of things. The hemlocks in our

grove are not all dead. And yet this forest in Petersham, Massachusetts, is dying and telling our little group as much when we look
around—but also when we listen.

The hemlocks that remain are about to offer their own eulogy, a
remembrance of their species, as the species leaves the earth. We
only have to listen to what the hemlocks have to say. Don't worry—I
am not saying the trees are talking or, more worryingly, that I *hear*
the trees talking, though I would be lying if I said I had not done
quite a bit of talking to trees. I'm saying I hear the sound of the
hemlock trees as they stand dying, a sound I will describe in just
a bit. And hearing hemlocks brings me back to questions we face
when a species of tree is leaving: What do we do? What has happened before? Are we ready to bear witness?

I'd been to hemlock groves on many occasions, but I'd never
really listened to a hemlock forest before. I was amazed, frankly,
and I carried what I heard all the way home with me like a catchy
tune or something important someone had said. I heard it on the
walk from the woods back to my car and on the drive back, when
the windows were down and the highways moving, when the windows were up and the traffic bad. Sure, I turned on the radio some,
and I got out of the car and bought some coffee at a rest stop and
at some point I listened to the traffic report—as I passed through
various eastern cities, small and large, seated on big rivers that had
themselves been charged, in a distant way, by little streams that had
been cooled by hemlock groves to the north—but I could still hear
the hemlock, and still can.

Like traffic, the hemlock is not sexy. It is not a celebrity tree, one
of the reasons I admire it and often think of what it said. It is an

uncelebrated tree in the not-so-celebrated forests of the Northeast—that is, the non-West. Hemlock is no sequoia, with its own national park. Even when hemlock was thriving, it was never expensive, nor coveted by woodworkers the way a woodworker would covet walnut or oak. New England fishermen used its bark to dye their sails and nets. John Josselyn, an Englishman who lived in the colonies for a few years and published *New England's Rarities Discovered* in 1672, noted that hemlock's turpentine was good for "any Ach." Hemlock tea, it turns out, is high in vitamin C, and, to return to our theme, anything in any way associated with the common cold is just not sexy.

The eastern hemlock's humble reputation may also have to do with its habitat, which is vast but out of sight. If absence makes the heart grow fonder, the opposite applies to hemlock: it grows in swamps and rocky slopes and deep ravines north into Nova Scotia and New Brunswick and west into Quebec and Ontario, and then stretches out to Michigan and Wisconsin. In the South, hemlock extends into Georgia and Alabama, as if following the Appalachian Mountains. (Charles Sargent's classic monograph on hemlock marks the southern reach of hemlocks at Clear Creek Falls. Those falls, like the hemlock of Alabama, are gone, flooded by Alabama Power in 1961, subsumed by the current Lewis Smith Lake.) Hemlock tends to grow in the faraway places that are close in. Like nature in our mostly urban lives, it is ubiquitous but can seem to be at a distance.

To a woodworker, hemlock is knotty, coarse-grained, brittle, shunned even as a Christmas tree, the needles fallen as soon as the tree is set up indoors. If woodworkers turned to hemlock, they did so for pallets and boxes, crates and shingles, lathings and paper pulp—stuff we stepped on, shipped, jotted on, and crumpled. Loggers were advised to sell it fast and cheap, as railroad ties. I like to think of all the trains that went west on hemlock after the eastern forests were cut over: over the prairies and the West Coast, to cut down the next forests. A pulp mill on the Olympic Peninsula, Rayonier, helped develop rayon—an inexpensive synthetic alternative to silk—in 1931 with the pulp of western hemlock, a distant relative of the eastern hemlock from back when the continents were lined up differently. (*That* hemlock is immune to the ravages of the hemlock woolly adelgid.) The Amish used hemlock for framing, and a building roughly made might be covered in hemlock, built with long-lasting hemlock floors, and hemlock-sided. Given all the tannin in the bark, hemlock siding lasted, and after hemlock is dead and gone, it will be interesting to see how long its remains linger on the forest floor.

Over the course of its role in the daily life of humans, the hemlock's most famous use was in tanning, thanks to its thick, reddish, tannin-rich bark. Animal skins were soaked in hemlock-infused baths. Anyone who has ever fly-fished in the Schoharie Creek in the Catskill Mountains has considered the shade-scarce banks of the creek compared with what they must have been before Colonel Zadock Pratt Jr. moved to Schohariekill to build what was, in 1840, the largest tannery in the world. Pratt chose Schohariekill precisely for its hemlock. Old majestic groves surrounded the town in steep ravines—so steep that the area is now surrounded by ski resorts, giving you an idea of the kind of terrain that hemlock loves. As Prattsville built up, it was soon referred to as "The Gem of the Catskills." In *The Catskills: From Wilderness to Woodstock*, Alf Evers describes the procession of skins that were brought in from around the world—from California and Argentina, from Honduras and Uruguay—to Pratt's swamp tannery to be turned into shoe leather. The trees were skinned by gangs of workers called "peelers," and entire slopes of barkless trunks were left to rot.

Pratt served two terms in Congress, founded a bank that printed its own currency with his image on it, and had scenes from his life depicted on a cliff above the tannery. He also had his cranium measured by a phrenologist, who described Colonel Pratt as "extravagantly organized." "He is from these causes, consequently eccentric," the phrenologist continued. "Each action and motion bears the impress of his mind, which makes him somewhat peculiar, isolated and detached from his species." Pratt married five times. Three wives died young; the fourth divorced him. The fifth worked in the office of the tanning industry's newspaper, the *Shoe and Leather Reporter*, the editor of which claimed the final Mrs. Zadock Pratt had, in his words, "acquired that amiability and flavor of The Swamp that made her attractive to the old tanner."

Pratt aspired, in his words, "to live with the local people and not on them"—though he eventually managed both. As dead trees littered Prattsville, Pratt hatched a post-hemlock plan based on the theory that forested "hemlock land," used for dairy production, made for great butter. But the world's largest high-quality butter town never happened. By 1845, all hemlocks within a ten-mile radius were gone, and the town quickly shrank. Pratt commissioned himself a hemlock coffin. In the Catskills, it was well noted that a green hemlock log thrown on a fire crackled like a gun battle. "And when I die let me be buried in a hemlock coffin, so I'll go through hell snapping" was an oft heard refrain. Shortly before he died, a flood washed Pratt's coffin down the Schoharie Creek. In 2011, Prattsville suffered another disastrous flooding, this time the result of Hurricane Irene. It might not have been so bad had Pratt never set up shop, or had he moved to butter sooner, or just further considered the implications of cutting so many hemlocks along steep ravines. A little forest management goes a long way.

In preparing for the hemlock's eulogy, it is important to remember that a striking characteristic of human civilization is its tendency to discount what is most essential to sustaining its long-term existence. Swamps, for instance, are forever being filled in—or "reclaimed," the old real estate term for dumping garbage in a marsh. The word *reclaimed* implies that it's always for civilization's betterment, even if civilization would be better off if the watery guts that clean and nourish our rivers and streams were not filled in.

In my mind, a hemlock forest is the upland equivalent of the undervalued salt marsh at the distant bottom of a stream, a place that gets along despite the encroachment of humans surrounding it, a place often a little bit neglected by the powers that be (due to its economic unsexiness, its out-of-the-way-ness), even though locals, the people who know it best, often cherish it. Like an old swamp in a city, it is a place that, when engaged with, helps the humans get along a little better. Forests, like salt marshes, offer us chances at long-term relationships with a landscape, especially when we tie ourselves to them as a resource—an economic, ecological, and sure, even emotional resource—and especially when we allow them to be forests.

What's important about a hemlock forest—and what makes its demise important to regions beyond the eastern forests and the boreal forest that covers 1.4 billion acres across most of Canada—is that hemlock is a foundation species in the forest. Losing hemlock is like losing a conductor *and* the music, though rest assured the concert hall remains, and there are plenty of people waiting in line to play.

The hemlock forest we will hear eulogize itself today is quiet and dark, like a hemlock forest, and it began sprouting around the time Dolley Madison was first lady. And these are *young* trees, relatively speaking. Some of the oldest hemlocks are close to five hundred years old and are still standing in the least touched places in the East, like the Berkshires in Massachusetts and the Adirondacks in New York. But many of them have already fallen—just look at the dying groves in Great Smoky Mountains National Park. I hate to separate the country from the city, or call one thing natural and another thing not, but to put it in terms of urban ecology (which to me is related to rural ecology but with higher rents), the rare, old hemlock woods that remain are like the city trees in abandoned lots, or that old retired guy in the last rent-controlled apartment, surrounded by gentrification, holding on, until now.

It had been hot in New York City when I drove out in the morning to pay some final respects to the hemlocks. But when I stepped into the hemlock forest, the temperature dropped; it was immediately and blessedly cooler by ten degrees, like an old church in summer. The hemlocks I went to hear are in the New England uplands, and I made the drive in part because the hemlocks in the city where I live and in the coastal lowlands are already gone. The Hemlock Forest, a fifty-acre grove in the New York City Botanical Garden—once a cool, quiet place along the Bronx River—is no longer hemlocks. Likewise, most of the hemlocks on Hemlock Hill at the Arnold Arboretum in

Boston have fallen to the punctuation-size aphid-like insect.

The hemlocks on Hemlock Hill were famously visited by the transcendentalists, notably Margaret Fuller, the transcendentalist newspaper columnist who wrote for the *New York Tribune*. Although the Great New England Hurricane of 1938 knocked down dozens of the trees, the grove survived, but the few that remain post-adelgid are Chinese hemlocks planted near the top of the hill. The hemlock-less peak of Hemlock Hill—now a dry, rocky outcrop—is an off-the-manicured-path kind of place that attracts another kind of transcendental experience. The last time I was there, I saw evidence of a high school outing—that is, empty beer cans. High schoolers like to be just out of reach of the authorities, the way old-growth hemlocks tend to be just out of reach of the ax.

Another transcendentalist who stumbled on some old hemlocks in his own backyard was Henry David Thoreau. Thoreau climbed Mount Monadnock, just over the border from Massachusetts, in 1844, 1852, 1858, and 1860, always botanizing, always taking notes. Monadnock wasn't wild and unspoiled like the Maine woods where he also explored; he liked it because it was an old place practically just out back, a pocket of wildness. It was hemlocky, I would say.

I thank Thoreau for leading me to today's eulogy. By my measure, the world is still a pretty good place if you can call somebody up and get invited to walk in some woods, and that's what happened when I first called up David Foster, director of the Harvard Forest. I was thinking a lot about Thoreau at the time, and Foster had written one of my favorite books on the forever misinterpreted Massachusettsian, *Thoreau's Country: Journey through a Transformed Landscape*. Foster's book begins in the Vermont woods in 1977, Foster just out of college and about to build a cabin. With Thoreau's journals as company, Foster discovers a discrepancy between the thick New England forest of 1977 and the forest Thoreau described from 1837 to 1861. Thoreau, it turns out, lived at the peak of New England deforestation—not what we think of today when we think of Thoreau country. He lived among some woods but primarily farms and meadows. The pond-side woodlot where Ralph Waldo Emerson allowed Thoreau to build a cabin was an anomaly: ministers were paid in wood in Thoreau's time, the trees at Walden Pond being a little like an oil field in twenty-first-century Iraq. Foster's book helped me access that other time in the landscape, to imagine whole forests coming and going.

This is a trait I admire about foresters: they think big. Some of the greatest thinkers about the American landscape were foresters, including Gifford Pinchot, Aldo Leopold, and Benton MacKaye. MacKaye drew up plans to remap the entire U.S. during the Great Depression, and his Appalachian Trail is more than just a great trail; it is a model of locally administered regional planning. When I am thinking about rush-hour traffic, a forester is likely to be thinking about the last ice age, or the birch and oak that will be along a hundred years after a hemlock forest dies—or in the case of the ecologists at the Harvard Forest, a regional plan called Wildlands and Woodlands that seeks to keep our vast (and often forgotten) northeastern forest productive. Maybe this bigger picture has to do with the roots of the word *forest*, the place outside the king's garden, the place beyond.

A reason the Harvard Forest is a good place to pay your respects to hemlock is that the scientists there are maintaining vigil. They are using the thirty-five-hundred-acre forest to investigate, as their mission statement says, "the ways in which physical, biological, and human systems interact to change our earth." The place is also just a little nutty—no offense to the scientist working for decades on experiments that are changing our understanding of the landscape. There is a farm, the old Sanderson place, and walking trails through the postcard-perfect New England landscape almost everywhere you look. But hoses and towers and cameras and monitors also read the vitals of trees, inspect a grove's breathing. It's a wired forest.

And despite all the modern appliances, the eighty-year-old dioramas at the forest's Fisher Museum—eight beautifully crafted depictions of moments in the New England landscape from 1700 to 1930—are better than any 3D internet experience I've seen (trees made of copper wire, the smallest wire, the smallest limb). They tell the story of a forest that, since European settlement, was cut and ·cleared, grew back, was cut again, and now, and its latest rendition— targeted less by axes and more by invasive species and development— is a system we need more than ever in a warming global environ- ment. A fact I repeat to anyone who will listen: when spring comes and the trees in New England burst forth their leaves as part of the larger eastern forest that runs from Canada to the Carolinas, from New York to Ohio, more carbon is sucked out by the forest in and around New England than by the Amazon forest.

As the woolly adelgid moves north with warmer weather, as hemlocks die, what will happen to the forest? Will it still suck as much carbon, for instance? These are questions the Harvard Forest is poised to answer as the loss of a foundation species is measured more fully than ever before. Measuring and analyzing the collapse is like having a seat at the big bang, a view of a disruptive event that will inevitably bring something new, new systems interacting in new ways. Understanding this kind of death is crucial to understanding how we shall proceed with life in a world where species are less and less a surprise.

A while ago I heard a woman in her eighties lament that she was at an age that meant spending a lot of time at her friends' funerals. This is our future as North Americans who live among old friends who are trees. In Minnesota, the warming climate—projected to raise temperatures about ten degrees by century's end—is expected to change the hardwoods and conifers that make up the boreal forest of the Boundary Waters into an oak savanna, featuring stunted bur oak and juniper, prairie grass, and prickly pear cactus. a scene from today's Kansas. State officials are attempting to plant themselves out of a decline, a move that is especially controversial around protected wildernesses like the Boundary Waters Canoe Area Wilderness and Isle Royale National Park. Is it right to put an old forest on life support?

At the Harvard Forest in Petersham, they are not replanting hemlocks, so a question sprouts: what will happen when hemlocks are gone? We can look at past declines, many of which teach us about what Bob Marshall, the Wilderness Society cofounder and Harvard Forest alum, described as the forest's "dynamic beauty." And we can make some predictions. At the moment, the woolly adelgid has a competitor as far as hemlock killing goes: in New England another primary cause of hemlock death is preemptive logging, before the adelgid gets to it. Studies of plots logged in the Harvard Forest to simulate preemptive cuts show us that a lot of carbon is released from the forest floor. Black birch, meanwhile, comes running in, happy to take hemlock's place.

If you are walking into a hemlock grove with David Foster and his colleagues, everything is put in relation to change. "In many ways you can just look at this as part of the natural flux of the forest," Foster said to me on the day I went to hear the hemlock's eulogy. "The trick in thinking of it that way is that this of course is an introduced species from outside the evolutionary history of the system." That's the woolly adelgid, who hails, as mentioned, from Asia. "And so it isn't a particularly natural part of this system," Foster went on. "But the way the forest is coping with it is the same way that it would cope if this were a native insect or a hurricane or a tornado or something else—the forest wouldn't get upset, it copes. In fact, the deer are quite happy. Lots of new shoots."

"There are winners and losers," said Steve Long, a longtime forest watcher. He is the founder of *Northern Woodlands* magazine, the author of *More Than a Woodlot*, and a student of the 1938 hurricane, an adelgidlike devastation whose damage is visible in the Harvard Forest, just as the earlier chestnut blight is visible: today a dead but still standing chestnut leans relaxed against a terminal hemlock. "Black-throated green warblers are here now, and they will go. The conifer structure is what they like."

If I were to jog out to this place in the forest a hundred years hence—I mean, if I am going to be alive in a hundred years, I might as well be in great shape—and then attempt to describe to children the hemlock forest that once stood on this spot (the cool shade, the darkness, the quiet), I would likely not be able to distinguish the onetime hemlock land from the rest of the forest. "Right now"—by which she meant today—"I would just jog in place," said Clarisse Hart, a forest researcher and a poet who works at the Harvard Forest. "The ground is so soft." And she's right. The lushness is what I ought to recall in that imaginary future: the softness of the ground, the smells—a smell she rightly described as "close and green." A sharper and more medicinal smell than a forest of fir trees. And then there are the smells of the moist hemlock floor itself and everything it grows: wintergreen plants that decorate the place, as well as a few feet of millions of needles, together offering a downlike softness of accumulated decay.

"It's sad," Hart added. She was talking about the death of hemlocks, and I agree, it is sad. And it is at this moment that Hart brings to my attention the sound of the hemlock grove.

The group that gathered here today is now standing still for a moment, getting ready to just listen. It brings to mind the kind of pause described in the first half of Robert Frost's poem "On a Tree Fallen Across the Road (To Hear Us Talk)." Humans naturally turn to poetry for help with loss. A good poet, after all, does what the forester does: takes in the myriad details to give us perspective, an entrance into a larger view of time. Frost writes:

> *The tree the tempest with a crash of wood*
> *Throws down in front of us is not to bar*
> *Our passage to our journey's end for good,*
> *But just to ask us who we think we are*
>
> *Insisting always on our own way so.*
> *She likes to halt us in our runner tracks,*
> *And make us get down in a foot of snow*
> *Debating what to do without an ax.*

Trees mark time for the humans who notice them, and in this poem the tree interrupts, diverts us into a suspended moment, what a musician would call a fermata. Frost is exacting. His metaphor unites with the natural detail; figure of speech and the reality of the fallen tree converge.

"Dust of Snow" is what I would call a very hemlocky poem that Frost published in 1923, while teaching at Amherst, which is, by the way, eighteen miles as the crow flies from Petersham. You can read it as a crow startling a man, a note of morbid awareness. But the power of the poem builds as you delve deeper into hemlocks. When you ponder what it means for a subdivision to punctuate forever a northeastern forest that perhaps you hadn't heretofore noticed, or what it means to end the regrowths and reincarnations of forests that lived previous lives as meadows around the time of Thoreau, or when you discover the efficiency of a hemlock forest—the need for so little light, the characteristic denseness of its canopy, branches from top to bottom, as opposed to, say, a pine, which concentrates its branches high on the tree, toward the sky—the poem grows on the forest-interested reader. Hemlock awareness changes your perception of the poem, and of hemlock. The hemlock-knowledgeable you becomes the poem's nurse log, primed for succession:

> The way a crow
> Shook down on me
> The dust of snow
> From a hemlock tree
>
> Has given my heart
> A change of mood

And saved some part
Of a day I had rued.

The hemlock canopy is a canopy that traps and holds snow, the hemlock growing so slowly as to be on an altogether different clock from that of the birch tree or the fast-growing pine, or the man standing beneath a crow. Nobody is sure how hemlock got its name in North America; there is only conjecture as to its resemblance to the plant called hemlock (although, more accurately, conium) that famously silenced Socrates, shutting down his nervous system gradually but completely. Nonetheless, it seems impossible to separate the hemlock tree from the hemlock plant's poison, for a poet to keep the death of Socrates out of the picture—for death is in the forest, especially a hemlock forest, especially now. But the dust of snow falls from one timescape to another, bridging a gap, adjusting distances and, thus, adjusting endings.

"You can hear it," someone in our little group says, and at first I think they mean the quiet.

I listen and at first think I hear the coolness, a stream of cold, rushing water. We look up, through the dense branches and millions of needles and the smallest pinelike cones. Like the dust of snow, or a touch of gray, we see evidence of death: the eggs of the adelgid, white woolly patches, cottony eggs that cover the trees' fine needles. Needles are brown, and on second glance more needles are white, the adelgids sucking away the old tree's life. In certain places in the canopy we see what we would not see in a healthy hemlock forest—light from above. (The light on a healthy hemlock-forest floor is 1 percent of the light entering the canopy.)

I keep listening to what I now understand is not a stream. This is the hemlock's final words, the sound of a thousand dying needles falling, a gentle rain, and it is steady. I can record it, memorize it, lock it in, and carry it home. A forest is leaving, going forever, at least our forever. And yet, when I play the sound back in my mind as I head off to sleep, I don't feel sad, though it is a sad sound. Death is sad, but death is not the end, especially in a forest. Emily Dickinson—who was as close as Frost to the hemlocks I hear today—suggested that a part of us leaves when a friend dies, but she also suggested an estuarine return:

> *Each that we lose takes part of us;*
> *A crescent still abides,*
> *Which like the moon, some turbid night,*
> *Is summoned by the tides.*

When I listen to the hemlock's sad rain, play it over in my head, I feel thicker, like a hemlock, more worn. I feel the still-cool air of the hemlock woods, and I imagine the ground, the cool ground of a forest that will once again undergo a change, a shift, a dynamic transformation that is like so many it has undergone over thousands of years of different lives—a high or a low tide, depending on how you look at it.

ALISON HAWTHORNE DEMING

The Web

—With lines from Claude Lévi-Strauss

Is it possible there is a certain
kind of beauty as large as the trees
that survive the five-hundred-year fire
the fifty-year flood, trees we can't
comprehend even standing
beside them with outstretched arms
to gauge their span,
a certain kind of beauty
so strong, so deeply concealed
in relationship—black truffle
to red-backed vole to spotted owl
to Douglas fir, bats and gnats,
beetles and moss, flying squirrel
and the high-rise of a snag,
each needing and feeding the other—
a conversation so quiet
the human world can vanish into it.
A beauty moves in such a place
like snowmelt sieving through
the fungal mats that underlie and
interlace the giant firs, tunneling
under streams where cutthroat fry

live a meter deep in gravel,
fluming downstream over rocks
that have a hold on place
lasting longer than most nations,
sluicing under deadfall spanners
that rise and float to let floodwaters pass,
a beauty that fills the space of the forest
with music that can erupt as
varied thrush or warbler, calypso
orchid or stream violet, forest
a conversation not an argument,
a beauty gathering such clarity and force
it breaks the mind's fearful hold on its
little moment steeping it *in a more dense*
intelligibility, within which centuries
and distances answer each other
and speak at last with one and the same voice.

WHITE OAK

JONI TEVIS

Acorn Bread

THAT FALL, my first October back in South Carolina, we had a bumper crop of acorns. Every day I heard the staccato rain of nuts hitting the roof, and when I walked the campus where I'd just begun teaching, acorns rolled underfoot. I'd read about acorn bread years before, and it seemed like a good time to try baking some, so I gathered nuts in a grocery bag until I had a good two pounds.

Shelling the nuts took all evening, but I found this strangely addictive. There's a trick to it—you pinch off the acorn's round top first, then its pointed end; after snipping through the shell, peel back the shiny brown jacket. When I found worms, I cut them out with a pocketknife. When a taste test proved the nuts were bitter, I boiled them in change after change of water to draw the tannins. I gathered white oak acorns; those from red oaks are more tannic. Squirrels, knowing this, eat white oak acorns out of hand but bury red oak acorns to use later. The soil's moisture leaches out some of the tannins, so the nuts taste sweeter when the squirrels dig them up—if they remember. And if they don't? Another oak seedling unfurls its leaves.

The boiling acorns turned the water dark, and rafts of steam rose from the pot. I roasted them on a pizza pan and ground them into meal with a food processor. Who makes acorn bread nowadays? Manna lying on the ground, free for the taking, but it's a lot of work.

As long as I can remember, acorns have caught my eye. Living pebbles you shine in your palm, tangible promise of new sprouts to come: willow oak streaked with sienna, overcup big as Gobstoppers, water oak packed with sunny yellow meat, bur oak capped with twisty fringe. Once, as a kid, I made an acorn necklace, carving holes in the seeds and stringing them on yarn. But when the crumbs of meal dropped to the ground, I regretted it. They would never become tall trees.

But I am older now, and calloused. If a tree can bear thousands of acorns in a season, as many do, eating a few pounds won't make much difference. Is this the attitude that wiped out passenger pigeons, once famous for their migration? That name synonymous with "moving about or wandering," flocks so great they dimmed the sun, nests so plentiful they split boughs; eggs dropped like hailstones. My loaf of acorn bread rose high and cracked in the middle; it tasted chewy, a little nutty, wild harvest on a suburban campus.

I think of other oaks I know, like the mighty *Quercus prinus* on nearby Table Rock. The crevices in their thick bark, deep enough for my hand to fit inside, mark their great age, as do their thick boles and tremendous height. They're likely the last few old-growth trees up there, rooted in ground stony and rough; that country used to be chestnut forest before the blight. Now that the chestnuts are gone, you wouldn't know they'd ever lived, but for the space their dying made.

Migrating flocks of passenger pigeons once left mountains of droppings, dark and rich, fertilizing ground that otherwise would have been too poor to support trees. Some of today's mature oak stands may have started with the help of pigeon guano, or the seeds the birds dispersed in the 1870s. It's possible that passenger pigeons gave my ridgeline oaks the boost they needed to survive.

It is good to return to a familiar place and find something sowed with a generous hand. The sun's energy translated into fat and fiber; I husked, baked, ate it for breakfast with smears of butter. What life I gathered and poured into my own. Even though the acorns had just fallen, some of them were sprouting already when I collected them, taproots poking from the meat's pale skin. Looking for cool damp, and tunneling down to find it.

WESTERN LARCH

Rick Bass

The Larch

A love story

For as long as I can remember having known them, I have been wanting to write about larch trees. I've been putting it off for fifteen years because, for one thing, it's like writing about lichens, or a clock that moves its hour hand only a fraction of an inch each year. (During my fifteen years of procrastination, one of the old giants has perhaps added only a half inch to its girth. And yet, magnified throughout the forest— millions of such inches—surely the power of glaciers has been equaled.) But also, I've simply been afraid of attempting an essay about the larch, such is the reverence I have for the tree.

They don't speak, not even in the wind, really—unlike the soughing and clacking limbs and trunks of the limber lodgepole, and the playing-card deck-shuffling clatter of aspen leaves in summer and fall—and even their dying comes slow. Sometimes a big larch will remain upright for a hundred years or longer after it's died—perishing in a huge fire or, occasionally, just dying, and finally rotting—and even after they fall over, snapping the other trees around them on their way and shaking the earth with their thunder, they remain there, solid and real, for centuries, and in many ways as alive, or more so, in their decomposition—possessing, or housing, more writhing life in that rotting than they did even in the upright living days of green and gold.

They are, of course, every bit as glorious in life as in death. While among the green and the living, they possess numerous attributes, one of the most underrated of which is that of water pump, intercepting snowmelt and surface sheet flow that might otherwise drain off to the nearest road and be carried away from the forest, unutilized. But larches capture and claim and hold within the forest that water, and they convert it to astounding height, and to magnificent breadth.

What else is the function of a forest, first and foremost, if not a place to do this: to capture and filter water, and merge with sunlight, to create intricate being, intricate matter?

The big larches don't just claim and hold that runaway water; they circulate it, too, each tree a miniature weather system unto itself, returning hundreds of gallons of water to the ecosystem each day in the form of transpiration, a fine, even invisible mist emanating from the needles, just as lung-damp breath is emitted from a man or a woman; and on cold and damp mornings, you can see the same clouds of steam rising in plumes from larch trees as you would see sifting from the mouths and nostrils of a forest of men and women.

This is not to say that larches are gluttons, greedsome water scavengers and totally out of control. One of the reasons they can get so big is that they can live so damn long, if you let them—if you don't saw them down. Around the age of two or three hundred, they really begin to hit their stride and, having clearly gained a secure place in the canopy, they can concentrate their efforts almost exclusively thereafter on getting roly-poly around the middle; and in the Yaak Valley, where I live, larches have lived to be six and seven hundred years old.

They can prosper with either seasonal or steady access to water, though they can prosper also on drier sites, such as those favored by ponderosa pine. When need be, larches can be prim and frugal with water, as in a drought, calibrating their internal balances with exquisite deftness to slow their growth as if almost into dormancy, where they hunker and lurk, giant and calm, awaiting only the freedom, the release, of the next wet cycle.

And they tolerate—flourish in, actually—fire, about which I will say more later.

Like any tree, they have certain diseases that can compromise their species—dwarf mistletoe, which sometimes weakens them through parasitic attrition, and larch casebearer beetle, which is kept in check by fires and by the incredible battalions of flickers and woodpeckers (pileated, black-backed, Lewis's, downy, hairy, northern three-toed, and more) that sweep and swoop through these forests, drilling and ratting and tatting and pounding, searching and probing and pecking and cleaning and aerating almost ceaselessly during the growing months. But for the most part, the larches remain relatively secure, in a world where so many other trees—fir, spruce, dogwood, oak, pine—are undergoing an epidemic of rot and beetles and blight and gypsy moths and acid rain.

Who can say for sure why the great larches are—for now—weathering the howling world so well, in these decades of such intense environmental degradation. From a purely intuitive level, I suspect that the answer has something to do with the larch's ancient jurisprudence—with the way it has evolved so carefully, so precisely, so uniquely and specifically to be safe in the world.

The larch is two things, not one: a deciduous conifer, bearing its seeds in cones but losing its needles each autumn, and it has selected the best attributes of each—the ancient conifers and the more recent deciduous trees—to fit into the one place on Earth that would most have it, the strange dark cant of the Yaak, tipped into a magic seam between the Northern Rockies and the Pacific Northwest.

Or, perhaps their sturdiness, their calm and elegant forbearance in a world filled with drought and fire and disease comes not from their wise evolutionary strategy of keeping one foot in each world, but from the fact that they lie so extraordinarily low, sleeping or near dormant for the eight or nine months of the year when they either have no needles at all (the first little spindly paintbrush nubs not sprouting out some years until May) or their needles have already shut down production and begun to turn bright autumn gold, which can happen as early as August. Perhaps, by sleeping so much, they age only one year to other trees' two or three or even four years.

In this regard, they are like a super-aspen, or a super-oak, calibrating their explosive leap of life to reside perfectly within that tipped thin window of sunlight and moisture in the Yaak, the three-month growing season, and then shedding their needles, just as oak and aspen drop their leaves, once that period of growth has ended, for there's no need to invest in keeping them, dormant or barely alive, through the winter. Better to shut it all down and sleep completely.

But larches are like a super-pine, too, or a super-fir, possessing the eager colonizing tricks of conifers that have flourished for the last eon in the huge landscape-altering sweeps of drama that follow the large fires in the Northern Rockies—casting their seed-sprung cones from high above, down into fertile ash, and in that way stretching like a living wave, or like an animal walking into new territory.

(In the Northern Rockies, some things run from a fire, and other things follow it—elk following the green grass that follows the autumn-before's flames, so that in one sense, perhaps as seen through squinted eyes, the elk can be said to be the grass can be said to be the fire, with very little difference in the movements of any of the three of them—all three generated and directed by the same force—and to that series of waves can be added the larch, colonizing those new burns and then reaching for the sky, rising slowly into 150-foot peaks that can take centuries to crest.)

So the larch, like the Yaak itself, is two things, not one: fire and rot, shadow and light. And in keeping with another of the stories of the Yaak—the fact that what is rare or even vanished from much of the rest of the world is often still present, sometimes in abundance, here—larches are the rarest form of old growth in the West, though in the Yaak, they are the most common form.

Biologist Chris Filardi has looked at maps of distribution for larch, as well as the habitat type found here, and has declared that the Yaak is "the epicenter of larch." This species is the one thing, I think, that is most truly ours. So many of the Yaak's other wonders are down to nearly the thin edge of nothing—five or six wolves, fewer than twenty grizzlies, a handful of lynx, a dozen mated pairs of bull trout, one occasional woodland caribou, a handful of wolverines, fourteen little roadless areas, one pure population of inland redband trout . . . The larch, however, are at the edge of nothing. This is the center of the center. Increasingly, I am convinced that the larch trees possess, more than any other single thing, the spirit of the Yaak.

Their interior wood, all the way through, is the red-orange color of campfire coals, a darker orange than a pumpkin, darker orange than the fur of an elk, and although I haven't found a scientist yet who can or will dare guess why the inside of the tree, never seen except when the tops snap off, or when the saw bisects the flesh, should be that firesome color, you would not be able to disprove, I think, the notion that there might be some distant parallel pattern or connection, out at or beyond the edge of our present knowledge, wherein fire likes, and is drawn to, the color of the larch's interior, for the larch is nothing if not birthed of fire.

And again, not just any fire, but the strangeness here, in the Yaak, of fire sweeping through and across a lush and rainy land that, when it is not burning, is rotting, and which is always, even in the rotting and the burning, growing—with seething, roiling life, and life's spirits, being released in every moment of every day and every night upon this land.

I have thought often that the shape of their bodies is like that of a candle flame. Broad at the base, measuring three, four, sometimes even five feet around, they maintain that barrel thickness for what seems like the entire rung of their length, before tapering quickly to a tip not unlike the sharpened end of a pencil.

This phenomenon is even more pronounced when their tapered tips get knocked off by wind or lightning or ice storms, leaving behind what now seems almost a perfect cylinder, and

which continues living, even thriving, without its crown—able
somehow to continue photosynthesizing and maintaining its vast
bulk by the work of the few spindly branches that remain. Sometimes only a couple such branches survive to nurture that entire
pillar, so that one is reminded of the tiny arm stubs of another
primitive, *Tyrannosaurus rex*.

There's some deal the larches have cut with the world, some intricate bargain, part vainglorious gamble and part good old-fashioned
ecological common sense. They've cast their lot with the sun rather
than the shade, having evolved to colonize new open space, such
as that which follows a severe fire, or patches of forest that are
infiltrated by slashes of light whenever other large trees fall over.
Because of this, they race the other sun-loving trees—the pines
and, to a lesser extent, the Douglas firs—for that position at the
canopy where they can drink in all of the sun, where they have to
suffer no one's shade.

But if they expend too much energy in that race for the sun—if
they channel almost all of their nutrients into the vertical component of height at the expense of the horizontal component,
girth—then they'll run the risk of being too skinny, too limber,
and will be prone, then, to tipping over in the wind, or snapping
under a load of ice or snow, or burning up like a matchstick in the
first little fire that passes through; and what good is it then to gain
the canopy—to win the race for that coveted position aloft—if
only to collapse, scant years later, under the folly, the improvident
briskness of one's success?

When the larch and lodgepole are found together, as they often
are up here, the larch will have been hanging just behind and

beneath the lodgepole for those first many years, "choosing" to
spend just a little more capital on producing thicker bark, both for
greater individual strength—greater static strength—as well as to
get a jump on the defense against the coming fires. It's always a
question of when, not if.

However, as lodgepoles begin to reach maturity and then
senescence, larches begin to make their move; and as lodgepoles
complete the living phase of their earthly cycle and begin blowing
over, leaving a larch standing alone now, the wisdom or prudence
of the larch becomes evident even to our often unobservant eyes. It
is then that the true glory of the larch is manifested.

Seventy or ninety or a hundred years old by this point, the larch
will have developed a thick enough bark, particularly down around
the first four or five feet above ground level, to withstand many if
not most fires.

And now, with competition for moisture and nutrients removed,
and the canopy more fully their own, the larch are free to really go
wild. They didn't have to outcompete lodgepoles for those first seventy or a hundred years; they just had to tag right along behind and
below. But now they can "release," as the foresters call it: having the
canopy to themselves, they continue to grow slightly taller, but now
pour more and more energy into girth, and into a thickening of
their bark—battening down the ecological hatch against all but the
most freakish, outrageous fires.

(So deep become the canyons and crevices, the corrugations of
that thickened bark, that a species of bird, the brown creeper, has
been able to occupy and exploit that specific habitat: creeping up
and down those vertical gullies, those crenulated folds a few inches
deep, picking and pecking and probing for the little insects that

hide beneath the detritus that collects in those canyons, and even building its nest in those miniature hanging gardens.)

Again, fire and rot are equal partners in this marriage, in this landscape quite unlike any other. And burn or rot, it makes no difference to the larch, really, how the lodgepole dies, for in their close association, the larch is going to feast upon the carcasses of lodgepoles, and assimilate those nutrients: either in the turbocharged dumping of rich ash following the fire that consumes the lodgepole but only singes the thick bark of the larch, or in the slower, perhaps sweeter and steadier release of those same nutrients from the fallen lodgepoles as they decompose. The forest will always burn again, but on occasion fire may not return until after that dead and fallen lodgepole has rotted all away, has been sucked back down into the soil and then taken back up into the flesh of the larch, the larch assuming those nutrients as if sucking them up through a straw—which, in effect, it does, through the miracles of xylem and phloem.

At this point, of course, it's off to the races for the larches. They just get bigger and bigger, in the manner of the rich getting richer. And they seem to put all of this almost ridiculous bounty—sometimes, literally, this windfall—into the production of girth; they pork out, becoming still more resistant to the perils of fire and ice and wind, so that now time is about the only thing that can conquer the giants, and even time's ax seems a dull gnawer against the great larches' astounding mass and solidity.

It could be said that the growth of lodgepoles represents reckless imprudence and a nearly unbreakable flexibility, while larches are all solidity and moderation. And if lodgepoles symbolize the dense connections of community, and the notion that when one is hurt or bent, all are hurt or bent, then larches are inflexible and isolate, loners, seemingly independent in the world and as rigid, in their great strength, as lodgepoles are limber—larches standing firm and planted, almost ridiculously so, in even the strongest storms, while all around the rest of the forest is swaying and creaking.

(Sometimes the force will be so great upon larches that they'll snap and burst rather than bend, and their top will go flying off, cartwheeling through the sky like a smaller tree itself, and afterward, the damaged larch will set about its healing, sending up a slender new spar or sucker in place of the old top, cautious but determined, and unwilling to cede anything, not even unto death— standing a century or longer, even after the life force has finally drained out of it.)

Western larch weighs forty-six pounds per cubic foot, dried, here in the Yaak; it's the heaviest, densest wood in the forest. It's like a cubic foot of stone, standing or fallen.

Often they're so heavy, so saturated with their uptake of nutrients, that on the big helicopter sales, in places so far back into the mountains, or on slopes so steep that not even the timber industry's pawns in Congress will have been able to appropriate public finances to build roads into those places, the sawyers will have to girdle the big larch trees a year or more in advance of the logging. This allows the life, the sap, to drain slowly out of the behemoths so that then, when the helicopters do come, and the girdled trees are finally felled, their dead or dying weight is considerably less than if they were still green, and the helicopter companies are able to save money on fuel because there's less strain on their engines.

As powerful and unyielding as the larch is, it only becomes more so as it ages. You can read the individual stories, year by year, in the

growth rings sampled by an increment borer or, in the case of one
of the giants being felled, in the cross section made by the saw and
sawyer. The spaces between the growth rings expand and contract
through the years, charting the individual's explosive early growth,
and then the slowing down, as if for a breath of air, and then, when
a fire or wind comes through and cleans out some competitors, an
expansion again, and to me such tales of thinning and thickening
read like the scan of a kind of silent music—a symphony of rise and
fall, contraction and expansion, segue and chorus.

Fire, ice, and wind: the larches' responses to and shapings
by these elements are dramatic, as is the flamelike alacrity with
which they leap from dormancy each spring, and with which they
retire for winter's slumber each fall—but I have to say, I think it is
their patience by which I am most impressed, and of which I am
most envious.

I want to believe they will be well suited to the coming temperature variations, the dormancy demanded not just by winter's
extremes, but by the coming heat and drought of global warming.
I know they lack the pines' flexibility, that they do not know how to
sway. Still, I believe in them, admire them, am in love with them.

And I dream of someone, one day, being able to walk from the
summit of the Yaak to the Canadian border in a swath of uninter-
rupted old-growth larch ten miles wide, as once existed, as evidenced
by the remnants still present, both standing as well as stumps.
I dream that someday a hundred years from now a traveler—
man, woman, child, or moose; bear, elk, wolf, or caribou—could set
out on a warm summer's day and pass through the leafy cool light
of an old larch forest, the duff soft underfoot and the air smoky and
gauzy with sun-warmed esters and terpenes emanating from the

bark, and the odor of lupine sweet and dense all throughout the grove—and that the traveler could walk and walk and never leave the old growth; could walk all day and then into the night, through columns of moonbeam strafing down through the canopy, and still be within the old forest; could pass out of this country and into the next and still be among those old trees.

The shape and nature and spirit of this land would accommodate such a vision yet. It is only up to our hearts to ask it.

I love the odor of them, I love the sight and touch of them. I love to lean in against them, to spread my arms around them, to touch the thick laminae of bark, to sit beneath them in storms while all else sways, as branches and streamers of moss whirl through the air.

I love to listen to the pileated woodpeckers drumming on them, and to the scrabble of little clawed animals scrambling up and down the bark of the living, as well as upon the fallen husks of the dead.

I love to see them lying on their sides in the ferns, rotting slowly—resting again, with the rain and sunlight still feeding somehow their magnificent and rotting bodies, even as they continue feeding the forest around them.

In their yearly dormancy as well, while losing the gold fire of their needles in autumn, they give back to the soil, particularly if a fire has just passed through, for the myriad wind-tossed casting of their needles acts as a net and helps secure the new bed of ash below, which might otherwise wash downslope and into creeks and rivers, scouring the watercourse and eroding the soil.

It is a beautiful thing to see in the autumn, after a fire, those gold needles cast down by the millions upon a blackened ground.

The two colors, black and gold, seem as balanced and beautiful as gold stars within the darkest night.

Late October and early November, after they have just gone to sleep, is the time I think of as being most their season. The sky above feels fuller in the absence of their needles. There is suddenly more space above, in a time when our spirits need that—in the dwindling days of light, and with winter's fog and rain and snow creeping in.

One night a damp wind blows hard from the south. In the morning the hills and mountains are covered with gold. It's an incredible banquet, a visual feast, and our eyes take it in all at once, and a thing stirs in our blood, a strengthening and quieting down both; and farther back in the forest the bears begin to crawl into their dens, seeking sleep also.

If the gold needles had stayed up there against that cerulean October sky forever, surely we would have eventually gotten used to them, and taken them for granted.

Hiking down off a mountain from far in the backcountry, I stop at dusk, weary, and without shedding my burdened pack take a seat on an old fallen larch, one of those ancient giants from the last century, its heartwood finally rotting but its outer husk still firm.

The immense log is covered completely with the gold confetti of its descendants growing all around it, and there is no table or other furniture I have ever seen more elegant or beautiful than that impromptu bench, nor more timely—I was tired and needed a place to rest, so I sat down and it was there for me—and I sit there resting for a long time, watching the dusk give itself over to dark.

And just as there is no furniture that could be the equal of a fallen larch left in the woods to rot or burn at its own pace, or under the pace of this landscape that is so intensely its partner, surely there can be no gold-lined streets of heaven superior to what awaits the residents of this valley on a fine October morning after a night during which the wind has blown hard, when our dreams of a night sky filled with swirling, shimmering gold are exceeded only by the beauty of reality as we first step outside to see one more glorious season being born into the ceaseless and enduring world.

CECILY PARKS

Bell

This newness of snow. This boot-ringing
as the snow warms in the sun to crush. These holes
we wind around the witnessing pines. This
violation of white. This slowness of moose.
This counting of steps. This counting of scars
in the bark: the warty burl bulging low
on the trunk, the black-scratchings left
by a bear learning to climb. This counting
of sleeps between this country & the next country
we call home. These branches shucking off
the statuesque in avalanches of needles & ice.
This progress, as in the wind-scalloped snowmeadow
pretending to be moon. This love that sets us scrambling
over the map's last ridge, our red hoods bright
in shrunken sky. This metallic weather in which we
are the ore. This alder. These crimson-tipped willows
reverberating next to a river of turquoise ice. This
following the deep tracks of one coyote stepping
where another has stepped. This wilderness
that we trespass, burning like berries in the juniper
& becoming the air in the belfry.

SPRUCE

JOHN HAY

The Autumn Trees

A T AN EARLY DATE we established a strong precedent on this continent for putting trees outside of all regard but that of our material needs. White settlers in America cut down the greatest deciduous forests on Earth. Today, the value of trees for our society is still more economic and utilitarian than anything else. If I were to believe the newspapers (which are, after all, made of wood pulp), I would have to view them as mere commodities, hardly included in the realm of being.

But there they stand in their great endurance, intent on their particular habits of growth, expressing Earth's superior depths and age. This stubborn growth of theirs is part of an interchange that goes far beyond our immediate sense of things. Between a California sequoia that may live for a thousand years or more and a white birch in northern forests that only survives to the age of eighty or ninety lies an extraordinary range, not only of life spans, but also adaptability to this planet in all its changes and conditions. Trees are central to Earth's expression, in depths of silence, torrents of energy.

I once set out on a camping trip along the Deerfield River in
Vermont. We had made our way to the campsite through dark
woods, slipping over wet logs, fording stony streams, tramping over
shallow duff at the river's edge, while the wind kept increasing in
intensity. Along the route were a number of big maples, covered
with the yellow leaves of autumn, that made me very conscious
of their presence. They had been growing there for a long time,
stubborn roots probing piles of schist and a stretching skin of thin
soil, until they had attained eminence, affecting the character of
everything around them.

The wind grew wilder and the skies blacker. The waters of the
lake we were to camp by were whipped and torn, and finally inter-
mittent showers changed to full and uncompromising rain. We
packed up the tents and trekked back in the evening over trails that
had been turned into running streams. We skirted the river—deep,
wide, and dangerous—running down through woodland banks
with a drawing power of its own, full of torrents and torment; it
seemed to be gathering the growing darkness into itself. The wind
hit the maples that stood over it with a wild fury, so that their leaf
masses whirled like fire in the sky. The great storm, like the trees
themselves, heightened the expressive unity of the region, its
endurance, its stress, its ceaseless cohabitation. I was conscious of
a power of interaction there, of bright leaves sensing change to the
measure of ages, of dark leaves and decay, and of all the transmu-
tations unknown to me but carried by creatures in the soil that
moved in and for one another, and manifested in strange forms
like slime molds that moved on trees.

Trees stand deep within a kind of knowing that surpasses
human knowledge. We run too fast to be received by them. Going

too far beyond them is to lose the sense of a community that thrives on the unities of the world. Another day in autumn, I was climbing up Sunset Hill, which overlooks Lake Sunapee, New Hampshire, where my family had their home. (Sunapee, with various other spellings, such as Soo-ni-pee, was an Algonquin name for "wild geese.") A light rain was falling, coming in with a southeast wind. Most of the leaves on the trees had changed to copper, bronze, and brownish yellow, or they had eddied off into the wind. A pearly gray mist stole between the trees and hung over outcroppings of granite. The wind would occasionally push little shreds of cloud across the trail. I passed through a gaunt, dark belt of spruce trees with splintered arms. It had haunted me as a child; I had imagined wolves running through it. Now the spruces were filled with a slow-moving, sea-gray atmosphere.

As light rain fell through clearings and was filtered through the trees, the hill was changed through the life of water. Countless new adjustments, recognitions, and responses were going on around me, which I could not begin to be aware of. The hill received all outer weather with inner calm, and much art of its own. I watched while a junco, slate-gray and white like rocks and clouds, whisked and darted around in the underbrush and then alighted on a low branch of a spruce. I saw a raindrop suspend from a waxy needle in front of me, as it was swelling and about to fall. Water drop and junco, instead of being two separate and separable phenomena, became simply and easily allied. I was ready to say that a bird was like a raindrop. I felt that I shared a status in space with them, and blessed the rain for bringing us together.

The more we destroy the forests, the more we turn into sepa-ratists, strangers in our own home. We lose our way, because an age where all things are expendable makes it increasingly hard to identify what it is we need. You cannot follow trees if they are not in you, but only in your way.

Trees refuse defeat, growing back again, rooted in timelessness. They are grounded in the dark, while in their spiraling arrangements of leaves and branches, they aspire toward the light. What speech is there, you wonder, in their communion with the earth? At times you feel great glooms for which they, rather than mankind, bore the chief responsibility.

In their presence, you may become aware of a greater, planetary silence that defines the unknown, if only because it refuses to answer when invoked. I think of one midday that was turned into twilight during an eclipse of the sun, and of its incredible hush, deceiving birds into roosting in the trees. Standing in with universal process and its great events, the trees seem to ask us, What more do you need to know?

It may be that the less we are able to attribute to trees, the more impoverished we become; it is a kind of deforestation of the spirit. They have a suprahuman quality that cannot be diminished. No matter that the ancient belief of indwelling spirits in them seems outdated. Their least understood qualities lie in the sensate natures they share with the rest of life, and to which the realm of the spirit is never foreign or distant. When I look out the window at a cutover area where pasture birch, young sugar maples, or white pines are growing back, I know that they have a will of their own, an ability to return, which is more than automatic. I also sense that trees must be aware of one another. They must share in the whispered nature of their race. They are fellow communicants, though in ways I can only guess at.

I am encouraged to look further into the matter of spirit in trees. I confess that I have little rational proof, but I count on the magnetism of the wild, from which we both originate, to prove it for me. We have hardly started to explore those roots again. Eventually, we may learn to include the trees in our feelings for all the living, in mutual chemistry. We share their space, and have only to think of it as a privilege.

CHERRY

Katrina Vandenberg

Cherry Season

Taste and spirits passed down over centuries

I.

My mother's mother kept a set of painted wooden nesting dolls
on top of her television. When I was small and went to her house,
I would take the set apart and line up the five dolls on her living
room floor, side by side, from biggest to smallest. The biggest was
my grandmother's mother, Maria Florence, and next were my
grandmother, my mother, and me.

I never knew what to do with the smallest doll, the only one that
would not twist open and reveal her secret. I usually named her
after my sister.

Maria Florence hailed from a place where cherries grow wild,
a village between the current border of Alsace-Lorraine and the
Rhine River. The village is technically German now, but the area is
liminal, and who it's ever belonged to is fuzzy. The cherries of this
region are morellos, dark skinned, fleshy, and tart. They look sort

of like bings, the sweeter eating cherries that grow in the U.S., but smaller and less sweet.

Morello cherries were brought to Europe by the Romans, whose empire's eastern border was the Rhine River, and whose soldiers were given cherries as part of their provisions. It is said that you can trace the paths of old Roman roads through their former empire by following the growth of wild cherry trees. The soldiers spat the pits as they marched.

I love cherries. Given a pastry shop, given a choice, I would choose cherry streusel, cherry-filled bismarcks, cherry kolache. I love eating cherries out of hand, worrying the flesh from the stones with my teeth. So do my mother, my sister, my daughter. So did my grandmother, who lay awake at night, pregnant with my mother, craving cherries. So did Maria Florence, who would have grown up on her mother's cherry cake, cooked cherries simmered in red wine and cinnamon, drunk cherry liqueur.

I like to believe that I inherited from the women in my family a genetic disposition toward cherries—that cherry is a taste we nurtured over many centuries.

Other facts about the women of my family: Our hair never turns gray, except for one streak at the left temple. Each of us gets angry or passive at the very moment it would have been more useful to do the opposite. Each of us has said at one time or another that we did not feel mothered by our mothers. "I know my mother loved me," we all have said, "I just never thought she liked me much."

Cherries are members of the rose family, a sprawling group whose leaves are leathery and oval shaped, with jagged edges. Strawberries, blackberries, cloudberries, and raspberries are all members of the rose family. So are apples, pears, and quinces. Cherries are part of a subgroup within the rose family, the plums, and are the closest kin to apricots, peaches, nectarines, almonds—drupes, stone fruits with a single pit.

The flowers in the rose family are cup shaped, with parts that come in sets of five: five petals, five sepals, stamens in multiples of five. If you cut open an apple crosswise, you will find a star shape in the fruit's center, made from the seeds in the apple's five ovaries.

Store-bought cherries are expensive because cherries are fragile. They must be harvested by hand, and the harvest itself is chancy: their skin absorbs water, and too much rain can make them burst. I've stood at my kitchen window and watched an entire summer's crop on our tree be ruined by a single downpour. If they're not ruined immediately, any rainwater left in the bowl of the fruit, that little dimple at the base of the stem, will soon cause the skin to crack.

The scientific name for cherries is *Prunus avium*, "plums for the birds."

Cherry season represents the heyday of summer, and is said to be a couple of brief weeks. But my experience, based on the dwarf tree in my backyard, is that cherries are only ripe for picking for a week at most. In the spring, our tree is foamy and laced with blossoms, filling our kitchen window. We get a few days dizzy with white flowers and their pale yellow stamens, and then, eight weeks later, another few days dizzy with red fruit.

In folklore, the presence of cherries is always interlaced with the idea of fleeting time and a season of pleasure, a gift that is given and then gone. Beyond the hundred-year-plus association of cherries and female virginity, there's an unlikely history between cherries and cuckoo birds. Like cherries, birds in general are strongly associated with the passing of time, and with change—probably because of the ways their migration patterns mark points in the wheel of the year, and how they sing at specific times of day. So birds have always decorated mechanized clocks; roosters especially tend to adorn clocks in cathedrals. But cuckoo clocks were first designed in the Black Forest, near Alsace-Lorraine.

It is said that a cuckoo needs three good meals of cherries before it can stop singing. That a cuckoo perched in a cherry tree can tell the future. If you chant *Cuckoo, cherry tree, please won't you tell me, how many years until I die*, the number of times the cuckoo sings back is the answer.

In a medieval play, a pregnant Mary and Joseph are walking by some cherry trees. Mary craves cherries, and asks Joseph to pick them because they're out of reach. Joseph, still bitter, tells her to ask the guy who knocked her up to do it. A moment later, the trees all lower their branches.

One afternoon when my sister and I were children, my mother took us to a cherry orchard with her. The farmer invited only my mother to climb the ladder. I sat on the ground and played with my sister, near tipsy bees sucking on smashed red fruit and the slowly filling cardboard flat. I remember the sight of my mother's legs on one rung, the rest of her vanished into the leaves, and the man smiling up at her, his chores forgotten. Everyone liked to talk with my mother.

At the end of the day, my mother allowed me to climb the ladder while the farmer wasn't watching. I hoisted myself up a few rungs until my head was in the canopy of leaves and clustered fruit and filtered light. I remember the leathery leaves, and how my mother and sister disappeared so quickly.

The tree muffled all the sounds of the neighborhood. All you could hear were the wind and the shuffling of formless color. I wrapped my hand around one of the branches crisscrossing what I could see of the sky. The bark was smooth and gray, with a series of small scars. I felt vulnerable and very alive.

Recently, I asked my mother about that day. *What orchard did we go to?* She smiled. *I bet that was at Aunt Teressea's house,* she said. *Really?* I asked. She grew confused. *I don't know,* she said. *I just don't know.*

2.

My mother's memory has been growing increasingly erratic for years. Then, a few months ago, she had a double brain aneurysm, and one of them burst. In one moment, she was talking to my father as she wiped down the kitchen counter with a sponge; in the next, she developed a terrible headache and forgot how to walk.

She had brain surgery twice, and learned to walk again. Then she came home. She still has trouble judging how far away she is from objects, like a chair she would like to sit in. But she retains most of her older memories and all of her quick wit.

The part of her brain that was flooded with blood and permanently damaged is the amygdala, which takes its name from the

Greek word for almond. It's the almond-shaped section of brain that processes memory and emotion.

In the literature our family was given, memory problems are referred to by a more clinical name: dementia. The aneurysms are described as looking like berries on stems.

My mother is not actively dying, so when she asked me to start working on a eulogy for her memorial, I felt unprepared. There still were infinite versions of her, infinite stories to tell.

For example: My mother taught fifth grade and had a reputation of being tough, fair, and fun all at once. She got on well with boys, especially ones usually labeled as problem kids. Our house was the sole one in our neighborhood that was never egged, that never had its Christmas lights broken.

Or: Her yellowed paperbacks were stacked on every surface in our house. They entered and left the house by the bagful. Beginning when I was ten months old, she took me in a stroller to the library for ten new books every ten days.

Or: My mother made cutout sugar cookies for us to bring to our class every holiday, hearts and shamrocks and pumpkins. She cut flowers from her garden, wrapped the stems in a damp paper towel and then aluminum foil, and instructed my sister and me to give the bouquets to neighbors, our piano teacher, our bus driver, anyone she thought needed a lift. She made a point of befriending janitors and secretaries, people others often dismissed.

Or: My mother was not blessed with patience. Once, when my sister and I had not cleaned our room, she threw a doll cradle against the wall and broke it. Another time, when I had left my bicycle parked behind her car in the driveway and she was late for a PTA meeting, she banged so hard on our side door that she smashed the glass with her fist. She made us lie to our father about how it happened.

Or: My mother was terrified of amusement park rides. My sister and I did once cajole her into riding a kiddie roller coaster with us. We laughed when she cried.

No matter what, when I write about my mother, I am cherry-picking, and picking cherries does not enjoy a good reputation. One dictionary says that to cherry-pick is *the practice of choosing and taking only the most beneficial or profitable items, or the deliberate practice of presenting only the ideas that support a preexisting narrative.* It is selfish, inaccurate, and frowned upon. To pick cherries is to distort objective truth for one's own gain.

Is that all I do when I remember—cherry-pick?

I used to have a massage therapist named Jim who was as much a spiritual advisor as he was a bodyworker. He had spent a decade as part of a semimonastic order in Germany, and when the order dissolved, studied with a healer in Denmark. When I asked a question like, Do you think you're doing the right thing? he would answer with a cryptic, *I don't think, I do.* He often said, *It's perfect the way it is.* One time he told me to look at my mother, my mother's mother, and as far back as I could in my matriarchal line. I was to think of what all of us had in common, and something we had all left undone. *That's your task,* he said.

3.

Maria Florence came to Michigan from Alsace-Lorraine as a teenager and eventually married another immigrant. (We never refer to him by name, only as "The Prussian.") They had a farm with cows and a herding dog named Shep. They planted a garden and lots of fruit trees and built a grape arbor. Every summer they canned and pickled over three hundred quarts of fruit and vegetables—tomatoes, cucumbers, cherries, and beans.

Maria Florence and The Prussian did not care for alcohol. Yet they made a wine press, and they thought nothing of making wine and fruit alcohol illegally through Prohibition. They drank one small glass every morning with breakfast, believing it to be a tonic for health. Kirschwasser, or kirsch, is a whole-fruit liqueur, by which they mean that some of the cherry stones are ground with the fruit as part of the mash. This is done to make the liqueur more complex, a little bitter and almond flavored, instead of sickly sweet.

Kirsch was created by monks in Alsace-Lorraine. It is considered eau de vie, or "water of life," because it was first created in the hope that it would cure sickness. The etymologies of the words for many other types of alcohol, like *vodka* and *whiskey*, involve the words *water* and *life* as well.

I lived in France for part of my college years in the city of Tours, where I studied language and literature. I used to eye the bottles of eau de vie in a shop window on my way home to my host family. The bottles were jewellike, with important-sounding contents and handwritten sepia-toned labels. The most beautiful of them was the Poire Williams, a curvy bottle with a soft fat pear in the bottom.

One day I went into the store to ask the shopkeeper about the Poire Williams. He tried to convince me that the glass blower forms the bottles around the fruit—*mais oui, mademoiselle!*—but finally admitted that the farmer ties the bottles to the branches over the pears while they are still buds, creating *des serres*, hundreds of tiny, perfect greenhouses, all over the trees. (I imagined dozens of bottles hanging from a tree, tinkling like wind chimes, but I would come to learn that the farmers wrap the bottles in burlap sacks to prevent breakage.)

Once the pears are ripe, the farmers remove the bottles from the trees, wash them, and fill them with brandy.

The shopkeeper declared, *Il faut que vous mangiez la prisonnière!* I must have looked baffled—the prisoner?—because he pulled a long, thin knife from behind the counter, then mimed sticking it down the bottle's neck, slicing, and spearing out slices of pear. Then he shrugged, smashed the invisible bottle, and rinsed his hands of the sticky invisible shards.

I imagine my gestating self as a pear in a bottle. All my life I've felt bound by an invisible form—able to see outside myself, imagining the ways I might be different, but never actually able to change in any significant way. There are times when I feel that I have been shaped from my beginning. Only a few years ago, after I had a daughter of my own, did I start to feel more at peace with the image.

Not everyone needs to become a parent to achieve perspective. But I did, and further, I needed to have a daughter. Once I became her mother, my body knew how fiercely my mother loved me. I could eat her up, even on the days when I'm bored or annoyed. Go ahead and roll your eyes. But why bother? At age eight she does so herself. She dodges my kisses, which I am told are *sort of gross*. There is always this separation, though, a pane of glass—which, if I'm being realistic, might only be a healthy sense of *self.*

I don't think my husband and I have ever used the word *choice* this much. *Make a good choice,* we say about everything from staying calm when being asked to put on pajamas to selecting healthy snacks. We emphasize her power to create her world, get along, succeed, find happiness.

But I also see what my daughter cannot. She has my eyes, but John's mother's nose and chin. She opens her mouth and tells me a wish she has, and it is word for word one my sister expressed at her age, forty years before. And this hope is an idiosyncratic one, something my daughter could not possibly know my sister ever desired.

Inside every question I have about mothers and daughters, I find another. They open and open into infinity, as in the poem "A" by Henrik Nordbrandt: *Already in the word's first letter / the word already is there / and in the word already, the whole sentence. / In the sentence are sentences / as the almond tree is in each almond / and a whole almond grove in the tree. . . .*

4.

When my mother was being treated for her aneurysms in the ICU, my father and I drove to the hospital, and he told me his theory about death and family. *When you're born,* he said, *it's like they put you on a ladder. All the people in your family who are older than you are a few rungs higher. Every time someone is born, or someone dies, everyone moves up a bit on the ladder.*

I do not wish to speak of my mother in platitudes. If it is true that funerals are for the living more than the dead, then on that day I would like to talk about my real mother. Funny and rowdy, fiery and fiercely loyal and prickly. Let us revel once more in my actual mother before we lay her to rest.

In my eulogy, I would talk about the way my mother delighted in possibility. I would describe the dinner during which she and my sister and I all lamented that we didn't like the names our mothers had chosen for us. My mother suggested that we all pick new ones, and so we did. We became Mary Nell, Rosemary, Cynthia. And when my father, Bernie, arrived home late and we all shouted, "Hi, Steve! he just shrugged and walked into the kitchen to make a sandwich. My mother held in her laughter, eyes daring him to ask.

I would talk about the December afternoon she sat at the kitchen table with my sister and me through the blue hour, teaching us how to cut snowflakes from folded sheets of paper. Her silver shears went *crunch sshh crunch sshh* like footsteps in the snow. The wonder of watching her unfold paper newly turned into fresh-cut snowflakes, over and over.

Most of all, I remember the day with the cherries, and how, before we went home, she let me climb the ladder into the tree. How that sudden shift in perspective she allowed me became a tiny and dizzying moment of transcendence. And how those few minutes kept opening and unfolding for the rest of my life.

I am in my late forties now, and I stand where she stood, half-seen in the trees. I am finally learning what it is to be an adult, to have a mother, to be a mother, to lose a mother.

Here's another thing about eau de vie: it's fermented, then double-distilled. If alcohol is created through distillation, it's referred to as a *spirit*.

The meaning of spirit as being simultaneously a kind of alcohol, a soul, an essence, and a part of the Trinity happens in a roundabout way. It all starts with the Arabic word for eyeliner, *al-koh'l*, which once upon a time was a fine powder created through a process of sublimation.

Alcohol became a more general term for any distilled substance, because the process of making eyeliner looked a little like distillation. Eventually, *alcohol* or *spirit* came to mean something pure, an essence released by the distillation process from the physical, or *the more gross,* as one sixteenth-century Brit explained it.

—and anyway, I keep wondering: how do you capture, *really* capture, the spirit of a person on a page?

5.

Multiple women across generations in my family are said to have visited one another as ghosts.

My great-grandmother died in a bed at my grandmother's house in late August 1936, only a few days before my grandmother gave birth to her first child, a daughter. My grandmother claimed that while she and my grandfather were in the bed holding their newly born girl, the ghost of her mother appeared in the doorway, dressed in her nightgown and smiling at the three of them.

I used to wave off this story as post-birth delirium, but my grandfather saw it too. He said, *Go back to bed, Mother,* and the ghost of Maria Florence disappeared and never returned.

The stroke that killed Maria Florence might have been an aneurysm. The condition is hereditary and most common in women.

The night before my grandmother died, nearly sixty years later, I dreamed that she and I were driving in her old station wagon, and stopped at a glass-paned greenhouse. She said to the man, *I'll take all the plants you have with yellow flowers.* The man began to pile them into her back seat. The back seat was soon full of yellow gladiolas, daffodils, rosebushes with their root balls wrapped in burlap, tulips, forsythia. It was too much. I told my grandmother to ask the man to stop. She said no, because she was leaving, and I needed the plants to have a happy life.

I woke, but was probably not really awake. It felt as though she were sitting on the edge of the bed, smoothing my hair the way she did when I was little. I was in school, eight hundred miles away from her. She was healthy. She had just sent me a birthday card with a check in it. The next evening her heart stopped.

Around the time my grandmother dropped out of high school to nurse her mother, who had stepped on a rusted spike and developed tetanus, the song "Life Is Just a Bowl of Cherries" warbled from radio speakers. The Great Depression was kicking in: increasing numbers of Americans were losing their jobs, major banks had begun to fail, and the singer asked, *The sweet things in life to you were just loaned, so how can you lose what you've never owned?*

Maria Florence stayed alive by drinking a mixture of whiskey and raw eggs through a straw. My grandmother never graduated, but kept her schoolbooks, Shakespeare's *Julius Caesar* and Tennyson's poems, until she died.

The one time I was really afraid for my mother's life in the hospital was when she started talking to her parents. They were in the room, she said. *Over there in the corner.* She looked at us as if we were incredibly dense. *Don't you feel the spirits?*

I can't imagine my mother's ghost smiling from a doorway or smoothing my hair. More than anything, my mother hates to be bored. When I came home alone from school, calling uncertainly from the doorway, "Mom? Are you there?" my mother would at times hide for several minutes before jumping from her hiding place, hollering bloody murder. I picture my mother's ghost doing something more along those lines. I was always so mad when she did that, but after a while I was glad to see her.

When I visit my mother these days, I like to go with her to church. As soon as the organ and processional start, her face relaxes and I feel her body grow more solid next to me. She remembers every word of the service. *Of all that is, seen and unseen.* My mother and I are seekers, though we never talk about that. The questions crackle in an invisible current between us: who are we, where do we come from, where do we go, how should we live? It is one more way in which my mother and I are alike.

I have picked out the verse I would like to read to her, near the end. It embarrasses me a little. My writer friends would pick someone like Hafiz, not Paul from the Bible. But it's the one I connect with my mother as my mother, perhaps because of the day in the cherry tree, or perhaps because of all the ways that parents so often seem unknowable to their children until after they die, at which point it seems they are revealed, but then become too slippery to grasp. *For now we see only a reflection as in a mirror; then we shall see*

*face to face. Now I know in part; then I shall know fully, even as I am
fully known.*

And did you know that neurologists used the scent of cherry
blossoms in an experiment on mice to prove that a memory's
effects could be passed down for multiple generations?

A couple of things I have inherited:

The hand-carved wooden box that Maria Florence carried across
the ocean in her steamer trunk. The box was made by her father
from a tree that grew near their house. My grandmother gave it to
me on the night I graduated from high school, and it was the only
time I ever cried while receiving a gift. My grandmother always
made me feel seen, in ways other adults never did. I loved the box's
jointed corners and imagining Maria Florence's hands on the lid,
and the forest full of cuckoo birds, where the tree grew. I loved
turning the small key in the lock and finding inside, again and
again, the letter from my grandmother, the two inexpensive pins
that her own mother once wore at her collar, and nothing else.

The pill I swallow every morning with my coffee. I also didn't
mention that all the women in my family have strong tendencies
toward worry and melancholy. But I happen to be the one who was
eighteen years old in 1989, the year the president declared that the
nineties would be known as "the decade of the brain," with a new
focus on neuroscience and pharmaceutical drugs for mood disor-
ders, so I am the sole one of us who holds a prescription, even as I
am nearly certain that we all share the same brain chemistry.

I keep emphasizing our likeness, but now I think this may have
been the problem all along. What if another way the women in my

family are all alike is that we *aren't* alike? What if that's what worried us as girls looking up at our mothers? What if all of us are like cherry trees, different and alike at once?

Or what if the task is not to worry? Now when I hear the phrase *neural pathways*, I picture the Roman soldiers walking near the vineyards, near the river, nearly two thousand years ago. The soldiers march through sun and shadow, spitting cherry pits, maybe fantasizing about dipping a chunk of bread in olive oil at the end of the day. The young men have no idea that these stones will become saplings, then trees, then more trees—that, thousands of years later, with the empire long gone and every one of their names forgotten, the ghosts of their paths will remain. That the people who live there now, some of whom share my blood, gather beneath those trees every summer. This goes on, generation after generation. They follow the line of trees without knowing where it goes.

ARTHUR SZE

Back-Lit

You pick the next-to-last apple off a branch;
here's to ripening, to the burr that catches
on your shoelace and makes you pause,

consider, retrace your path. The cottonwoods
have burst into yellow flame; by the ditch,
someone dumps a pile of butchered bones.

When we saw white droppings on the brick porch,
we turned and looked up to five screech owls
roosting on a dark beam, back-lit

through wisteria leaves. By the metal gate,
a bobcat bounds off with a rabbit in his mouth.
You yearn to watch sunlight stream

through the backs of Japanese maples;
but see now, sheet lightning in the dark,
it flows from your toes to fingertips to hair.

BUCKEYE

SCOTT RUSSELL SANDERS

Buckeye

YEARS AFTER my father's heart quit, I keep in a wooden box on my desk the two buckeyes that were in his pocket when he died. Once the size of plums, the brown seeds are shriveled now, hollow, hard as pebbles, yet they still gleam from the polish of his hands. He used to reach for them in his overalls or suit pants and click them together, or he would draw them out, cupped in his palm, and twirl them with his blunt carpenter's fingers, all the while humming snatches of old tunes.

"Do you really believe buckeyes keep off arthritis?" I asked him more than once.

He would flex his hands and say, "I do so far."

My father never paid much heed to pain. Near the end, when his worn knee often slipped out of joint, he would pound it back in place with a rubber mallet. If a splinter worked into his flesh beyond the reach of tweezers, he would heat the blade of his knife over a cigarette lighter and slice through the skin. He sought to ward off arthritis not because he feared pain but because he lived through his hands, and he dreaded the swelling of knuckles, the stiffening of fingers. What use would he be if he could no longer hold a hammer or guide a plow? When he was a boy he had known farmers not yet forty years old whose hands had curled into claws, men so crippled up they could not tie their own shoes, could not sign their names.

"I mean to tickle my grandchildren when they come along," he told me, "and I mean to build dollhouses and turn spindles for tiny chairs on my lathe."

So he fondled those buckeyes as if they were charms, carrying them with him when our family moved from Ohio at the end of my childhood, bearing them to new homes in Louisiana, then Oklahoma, Ontario, and Mississippi, carrying them still on his final day when pain a thousand times fiercer than arthritis gripped his heart.

The box where I keep the buckeyes also comes from Ohio, made by my father from a walnut plank he bought at a farm auction. I remember the auction, remember the sagging face of the widow whose home was being sold, remember my father telling her he would prize that walnut as if he had watched the tree grow from a sapling on his own land. He did not care for pewter or silver or gold, but he cherished wood. On the rare occasions when my mother coaxed him into a museum, he ignored the paintings or porcelain and studied the exhibit cases, the banisters, the moldings, the parquet floors.

I remember him planing that walnut board, sawing it, sanding it, joining piece to piece to make footstools, picture frames, jewelry boxes. My own box, a bit larger than a soap dish, lined with red corduroy, was meant to hold earrings and pins, not buckeyes. The top is inlaid with pieces fitted so as to bring out the grain, four diagonal joints converging from the corners toward the center. If I stare long enough at those converging lines, they float free of the box and point to a center deeper than wood.

I learned to recognize buckeyes and beeches, sugar maples and shagbark hickories, wild cherries, walnuts, and dozens of other trees while tramping through the Ohio woods with my father. To his eyes, their shapes, their leaves, their bark, their winter buds were as distinctive as the set of a friend's shoulders. As with friends, he was partial to some, craving their company, so he would go out of his way to visit particular trees, walking in a circle around the splayed roots of a sycamore, laying his hand against the trunk of a white oak, ruffling the feathery green boughs of a cedar. "Trees breathe," he told me. "Listen."

I listened, and heard the stir of breath.

He was no botanist; the names and uses he taught me were those he had learned from country folks, not from books. Latin never crossed his lips. Only much later would I discover that the tree he called ironwood, its branches like muscular arms, good for ax handles, is known in books as hop hornbeam; what he called tulip tree or canoewood, ideal for log cabins, is officially the yellow poplar; what he called hoop ash, good for barrels and fence posts, appears in books as hackberry.

When he introduced me to the buckeye, he broke off a chunk of the gray bark and held it to my nose. I gagged.

"That's why the old-timers called it stinking buckeye," he told me. "They used it for cradles and feed troughs and peg legs."

"Why for peg legs?" I asked.

"Because it's light and hard to split, so it won't shatter when you're clumping around."

He showed me this tree in late summer, when the fruits had fallen and the ground was littered with prickly brown pods. He picked up one, as fat as a lemon, and peeled away the husk to reveal the shiny seed. He laid it in my palm and closed my fist around it so the seed peeped out from the circle formed by my index finger and thumb. "You see where it got the name?" he asked.

I saw; what gleamed in my hand was the bright eye of a deer. "It's beautiful," I said.

"It's beautiful," my father agreed, "but also poisonous. Nobody eats buckeyes, except maybe a fool squirrel."

I knew the gaze of deer from living in the Ravenna Arsenal, in Portage County, up in the northeastern corner of Ohio. After supper we often drove the arsenal's gravel roads, past the munitions bunkers, past acres of rusting tanks and wrecked bombers, into the far fields where we counted deer. One June evening, while mist rose from the ponds, we count 311, our family record. We found deer in herds, in bunches, in amorous pairs. We came upon lone bucks, their antlers lifted against the sky like the bare branches of dogwood. If you were quiet, if your hands were empty, if you moved slowly, you could leave the car and steal to within a few paces of a grazing deer, close enough to see the delicate lips, the twitching nostrils, the glossy, fathomless eyes.

The wooden box on my desk holds these grazing deer, as it holds the buckeyes and the walnut plank and the farm auction and the munitions bunkers and the breathing forests and my father's hands. I could lose the box, I could lose the polished seeds, but if I were to lose the memories I would become a bush without roots, and every new breeze would toss me about.

 All those memories lead back to the northeastern corner of Ohio, where I learned to connect feelings with words. Much of the land I knew in that place as a child had been ravaged. The ponds in the arsenal teemed with bluegill and beaver, but they were also laced with TNT from making bombs. Because the wolves and coyotes had long since been killed, some of the deer, so plump in the June grass, collapsed on the January snow, whittled by hunger to racks of bones. Outside the arsenal's high barbed fences, many of the farms had failed, their barns caving in, their topsoil gone. Ravines were choked with swollen couches and junked washing machines and cars. Crossing fields, you had to be careful not to slice your feet on tin cans or shards of glass. Most of the rivers had been dammed, turning fertile valleys into scummy playgrounds for boats.

 One free-flowing river, the Mahoning, ran past the small farm near the arsenal where our family lived during my later years in Ohio. We owned just enough land to pasture three ponies and to grow vegetables for our table, but those few acres opened onto miles of woods and creeks and secret meadows. I walked that land in every season, every weather, following animal trails. But then the Mahoning, too, was doomed by a government decision; we were forced to sell our land, and a dam began to rise across the river.

 If enough people had spoken for the river, we might have saved it. If enough people had believed that our scarred country was worth defending, we might have dug in our heels and fought. Our attachments to the land were all private. We had no shared lore, no literature, no art to root us there, to give us courage, to help us stand our ground. The only maps we had were those issued by the state, showing a maze of numbered lines stretching over emptiness. The Ohio landscape never showed up on postcards or posters, never unfurled like tapestry in films, rarely filled even a paragraph in books. There were no mountains in that place, no waterfalls, no rocky gorges, no vistas. It was a country of low hills, cut-over woods, scoured fields, villages that had lost their purpose, roads that had lost their way.

"Let us love the country of here below," Simone Weil urged. "It is real; it offers resistance to love. It is this country that God has given us to love. He has willed that it should be difficult yet possible to love it." Which is the deeper truth about buckeyes, their poison or their beauty? I hold with the beauty; or rather, I am held by the beauty, without forgetting the poison. In my corner of Ohio the gullies were choked with trash, yet cedars flickered up like green flames from cracks in stone; in the evening bombs exploded at the ammunition dump, yet from the darkness came the mating cries of owls. I was saved from despair by knowing a few men and women who cared enough about the land to clean up trash, who planted walnuts and oaks that would long outlive them, who imagined a world that would have no call for bombs.

How could our hearts be large enough for heaven if they are not large enough for Earth? The only country I am certain of is the one here below. The only paradise I know is the one lit by our everyday sun, this land of difficult love, shot through with shadow. The place where we learn this love, if we learn it at all, shimmers behind every new place we inhabit.

A family move carried me away from Ohio thirty years ago; my schooling and marriage and job have kept me away ever since, except for occasional visits. I returned to the site of our farm one cold November day when the trees were skeletons and the ground shone

with the yellow of fallen leaves. From a previous trip I knew that
our house had been bulldozed, our yard and pasture had grown up
in thickets, and the reservoir had flooded the woods. On my earlier
visit I had merely gazed from the car, too numb with loss to climb
out. But on this November day, I parked the car, drew on my hat
and gloves, opened the door, and walked.

I was looking for some sign that we had lived there, some token
of our affection for the place. All that I recognized, aside from the
contours of the land, were two weeping willows that my father
and I had planted near the road. They had been slips the length
of my forearm when we set them out, and now their crowns rose
higher than the telephone poles. When I touched them last their
trunks had been smooth and supple, as thin as my wrist, and now
they were furrowed and stout. I took off my gloves and laid my
hands against the rough bark. Immediately I felt the wince of tears.
"Hello, Father," I said, quietly at first, then louder and louder, as if
only shouts could reach him through the bark and miles and years.

Surprised by sobs, I turned from the willows and stumbled away
toward the drowned woods, calling to my father. I sensed that he
was nearby. Even as I called, I was wary of grief's deceptions. I had
never seen his body after he died. By the time I reached the place
of his death, a furnace had reduced him to ashes. The need to see
him, to let go of him, to let go of this land and time, was powerful
enough to summon mirages; I knew that. But I also knew, stum-
bling toward the woods, that my father was here.

At the bottom of a slope where the creek used to run, I came to
an expanse of gray stumps and withered grass. It was a bay of the
reservoir from which the water had retreated, the level drawn down
by engineers or drought. I stood at the edge of this desolate ground,

willing it back to life, trying to recall the woods where my father
had taught me the names of trees. No green shoots rose. I walked
out among the stumps. The grass crackled under my boots, breath
rasped in my throat, but otherwise the world was silent.

Then a cry broke overhead and I looked up to see a red-tailed
hawk launching out from the top of an oak—a band of dark feath-
ers across the creamy breast and the tail splayed like rosy fingers
against the sun. It was a red-tailed hawk for sure; and it was also
my father. Not a symbol of my father, not a reminder, not a ghost,
but the man, himself, right there, circling in the air above me.
I knew this as clearly as I knew the sun burned the sky. A calm
poured through me. My chest quit heaving. My eyes dried.

Hawk and father wheeled above me, circle upon circle, wings
barely moving, head still. My own head was still, looking up, knowing and being known. Time scattered like fog. At length, father and
hawk stroked the air with those powerful wings, three beats, then
vanished over a ridge.

The voice of my education told me then and tells me now that
I did not meet my father, that I merely projected my longing onto
a bird. My education may well be right; yet nothing I heard in
school, nothing I've ever read, no lesson reached by logic has ever
convinced me utterly or stirred me as deeply as did that red-tailed
hawk. Nothing in my education prepared me to love a piece of
the earth, least of all a humble, battered country like northeastern
Ohio; I learned from the land itself.

Before leaving the drowned woods, I looked around at the ashen
stumps, the wilted grass, and for the first time since moving from
this place I was able to let it go. This ground was lost; the flood
would reclaim it. But other ground could be saved, must be saved,

in every watershed, every neighborhood. For each home ground we need new maps, living maps, stories and poems, photographs and paintings, essays and songs. We need to know where we are, so that we may dwell in our place with a full heart.

ALBERTO ÁLVARO RÍOS

Winter Lemons

Lemons in their second season, cold,
Yellow against the brisk night, bright,

Cold only fixing the color, crisping it,
Lemons in their gaudy, adolescent mustard

Lit in the heights of a late December morning,
Having climbed into the trees for sport,

Liking the dare: What did they used to be—mice?
Bigger. Rats, some of them, running up the trunks,

The branches—these are the bravest, the misbehaving
Boys, these lemons the rats nobody took home or let in.

The yellow of summer is not the yellow of winter.
The colors are the same but their stories tell two lives.

WHITEBARK PINE

Emma Marris

Handle with Care

The case for doing all we can to save threatened species

THERE'S SNOW on the ground, snow mist in the air, frost time on the mountain buckthorn. It is silent. On the ridge where I'm standing in Oregon's Crater Lake National Park, the snow outlines a stand of mature whitebark pine trees: huge, crooked, battered by time and ice, and covered in rough bark that here and there parts to reveal surfaces like polished bone.

Whitebark pine's ecological niche is the edge of existence. The trees are found on the highest, driest, coldest, rockiest, and windiest slopes. While lodgepole and ponderosa pine grow in vast stands of tall, healthy-looking trees, slow-growing whitebarks are tortured by extremes into individualized, flayed forms, swollen with massive boles from frost damage. Their suffering makes them beautiful.

But one can suffer too much. These pines are also simultaneously fighting two pest outbreaks. Jen Beck, Crater Lake's botanist, points out the characteristic orange buttons of an introduced fungus called blister rust and the sticky sap balls and pitch trails where the trees have in vain tried to defend themselves against ravenous bark beetles. Both the fungus and the beetle are believed to be booming, in part, because of climate change. These pines, perhaps six hundred years old and exuding the unmistakable venerability of ancient, distinguished trees, are dying.

I watch as Beck stoops over and, with a bare hand, sweeps away a few inches of snow to reveal a tiny whitebark seedling, no taller than her boot. Next to it, driven into the ground, is an unobtrusive metal disk bearing a number: 82.

With the help of a crew of colleagues and volunteers, Beck planted seedling 82 and several hundred others here in 2012. The seedlings all descend from cones collected from trees that seemed particularly resistant to blister rust. Seeds from hundreds of such cones were grown for two years at the Dorena Genetic Resource Center near Cottage Grove, Oregon, then exposed to the fungus and monitored for five years to determine how resistant they truly were. Seeds from the best performing cones were grown into seedlings and trucked to Crater Lake for planting. The hope is that they will speed up the spread of rust-resistant genes across the park—and that seedling 82 and its nursery-mates will help replace the dying trees.

The team worked hard to minimize the visual impact of its operation as much as possible. "It's not like they're out there in a grid," Beck tells me. "It isn't a tree farm." Each seedling was planted near a sheltering bit of rock or downed wood, both to shield it from wind and ice and to mimic the species' typical distribution. The metal tags were tucked under pine needles and a layer of soil.

And when seedlings die, as some inevitably do, the metal tags are carefully removed.

So far, Beck has planted her seedlings up to the very edge of the part of the park managed as wilderness. (Portions of Crater Lake have been proposed as specially protected wilderness areas since 1970, but the final designation hasn't come through. In the meantime, those areas are managed as if they were wilderness.) But now Beck wants to cross that line, to plant her custom-made seedlings inside that sacred space—an action that has raised eyebrows within the conservation community, but which she finds absolutely compatible with her work as a steward of Crater Lake.

To many, seedling 82 is a sign of hope, a gesture of care, and an act of responsibility on the part of a humanity whose understanding of its effects on the world is deepening. To others, though, seedling 82 is an unwelcome intrusion into a wild place, a living symbol of the arrogance of humankind and the assumption that we can control or fix disrupted nature. This is the view taken by members of a group called Wilderness Watch, who successfully argued to stop similar plantings in a wilderness area in Washington State. For them, planting trees as a gardener would challenges the self-willed spirit of the wild world. Meanwhile, half the whitebark pine in the United States grows in wilderness areas or areas managed as wilderness.

The determination to preserve "self-willed" nature is at the heart of our country's most famous branch of environmentalism, which found its roots in early preservationists like Henry David Thoreau and John Muir. With intellectual antecedents in Calvinism and Romanticism, traditional environmentalism's focus on the pristine married the assumption of a fallen humanity with a high value placed on freedom and the spiritual insight supposedly made possible by time spent in wild nature. In 1903, a few years before Theodore Roosevelt declared Grand Canyon a national monument, he urged Americans to "leave it as it is. You cannot improve on it. The ages have been at work on it, and man can only mar it." Much of the subsequent history of conservation was deeply influenced by versions of that sentiment. And although the conservationists who adhered to this way of thinking were not naive—they well knew the extent to which many of the lands they sought to protect were already altered by human beings—they still hoped to arrest and perhaps reverse the legacy of alteration. Their ideal was a wild space where humans were not in charge, where people could exercise their moral muscles and stand in humility before nature's workings, knowing and feeling their place as one species among millions.

But in 1995, in a widely read essay titled "The Trouble with Wilderness," historian William Cronon questioned pristine nature as a useful ideal. Seemingly untouched places serve as "the unexamined foundation on which so many of the quasi-religious values of modern environmentalism rest," he wrote. They form the "good" against which human civilization can be judged as bad. Deifying such places could be dangerous, Cronon argued: they could give us a false sense that we can walk away from our environmental problems and "escape history and the obligation to take responsibility for our own actions."

Today, our increasing awareness of the long history, massive scope, and frequent irreversibility of human impacts on the rest of nature make the leave-it-alone ethic even more problematic than it was in 1995. Climate change, land-use change, global species movements, pollution: these global forces affect every place, even those protected as parks or wildernesses, and dealing with them requires increasingly intensive intervention. The ecologist J. Michael Scott has been making a list of what he terms "conservation-reliant species"—those that need our active assistance to not slide into oblivion, and that will continue to need our assistance indefinitely. For these species, the threats to their existence will not go away, and people will have to hold their hands (or wings, or branches) perhaps forever to keep them alive. For example, the endangered Hawaiian stilt requires an ongoing program of controlling cats and rats, which have so far proven impossible to eradicate from the islands. The California condor only exists in the wild because conservationists periodically release more captive-bred birds. The Karner blue butterfly, the red-cockaded woodpecker, and the Kirtland's warbler now rely on us to set the periodic fires on which their habitats depend.

Thus a paradox has emerged: now and in the future, only natural areas with lots of human help will continue to look and function the way they did hundreds of years ago; land that is truly allowed to "go wild" will change in unpredictable ways. Suddenly the vacant lot in Detroit is wilder than Yellowstone, and a forest without white-bark pine might one day be wilder than one with it.

By planting rust-resistant pines, Jen Beck and the rest of the staff at Crater Lake hope to keep the park on the ecological trajectory it would have been on had not introduced fungus, climate change, and other human influences crossed park boundaries. But the park is managed in large part for the benefit of human visitors (and humans have interacted with the space for millennia), so there's a delicate balance to be managed. Beck canceled a planting that turned out to overlap with a "spiritual-use zone" identified by local tribes, and she lost some plantings near a road when a group of visitors had a snowball fight, knocking off the tops of a few seedlings. Meanwhile, she hopes to install a special paved trail so visitors in wheelchairs can see the whitebarks.

Still, many environmentalists seem wedded to the ideal of nonintervention once promoted by the likes of Thoreau, Muir, and Roosevelt. They do not support planting trees in wild areas, let alone more aggressive interventions, like moving species outside of their historical ranges to colder areas ahead of climate change. For them, the language of this new body of ideas about conservation, which frequently uses words like *engineer* and *manage*, lacks what environmentalism has always called for: human humility.

An entire book was recently released to counter the growing popularity of these ideas, the sum of which has been termed "new environmentalism." The promotional material for *Keeping the Wild: Against the Domestication of Earth* declares that, "with rhetorical fists swinging, the book's contributors argue that these 'new environmentalists' embody the hubris of the managerial mindset and offer a conservation strategy that will fail to protect life in all its buzzing, blossoming diversity."

The criticism of this kind of conservation—one that welcomes thoughtful intervention in natural processes—often hinges on the argument that without wild places as a guide, the work will lack a soul, an underlying ethic in service to life beyond our own species. It's feared that conservation will become a morally empty game, a project dedicated to rearranging bits of the natural world like Legos to create landscapes in service of humans.

But from the work I've seen at Crater Lake, in Hawaii, in California, and in many other places around the world, I've come to believe that the human attempt to save species and manage landscapes demands just as much from us, morally, as an environmentalism in thrall to wildness. In fact, it asks more. It asks that we sometimes give up our beloved wilderness and wildness to save other species. If we truly are the humble beings we strive to be, if we truly feel we are not more valuable than other species, then we must be willing to sacrifice our human-made category of "wild" for the betterment of those beings.

An environmentalism built around the pristine ultimately asks us only to leave, to withdraw. But today we can't withdraw without blood on our hands. The climate change we've fueled, the forests we've sliced into tiny fragments, the plastic we've heaved into oceans—so much of what we have done has the potential to drive species to extinction if we don't actively intervene to help.

An environmentalism built around nonintervention also perpetuates a false premise that humans don't belong in nature. And this mindset, this human exceptionalism, is itself arrogant. If humans are not exceptional, not morally superior to other species, not outside of nature, then privileging nonintervention over other environmental goals is deeply wrong—a version of fiddling while Rome burns, of backpacking while whitebarks die.

I would much rather see us do what works than what appears beautiful or feels good. We have to do whatever it takes to keep ecosystems robust and species from extinction in the face of things like climate change. And if that means that some ecosystems aren't going to be as pretty to our eyes, or as wild, or won't hew to some historical baseline that seems important to us, then so be it. We should put the continued existence of other species before our ideas of where or how they should live. Do Aldabra giant tortoises mind if, rather than dispersing seeds in the Seychelles where they are native, they do the same on Île aux Aigrettes off Mauritius, where they are playing the role of an extinct tortoise species? Are pikas fretting about raising their babies north of their native range, where they can avoid climate change–induced heat? Maybe, and maybe not. But don't we owe it to them to give them the opportunity to survive? Many endangered plants are thriving in cities. This doesn't mean we should abandon efforts to protect their native habitat. But also—why not?—plant them in TJ Maxx parking lots.

As we do our damnedest to save species, we can still cordon off some areas to learn how other plants and animals cope with changing conditions. These unmanaged areas will likely be transformed beyond recognition in our lifetimes, as new species move in, prairies become forests, fire regimes change, and so on. But we can't rely on them to protect all species, nor can we truly think of them as places beyond human intervention. These days, relinquishing our will to manage simply means throwing open the window and letting all the big, uncontrollable interventions—like climate change—come flying in.

Intervening certainly has risks. We don't know as much as we would like about how ecosystems work. We can't always predict when our meddling will save species or when it will backfire. But I believe we had better try. We've pulled a few species back from the brink—the California condor, the whooping crane—by insinuating ourselves in their lives as puppet mothers and migration guides, so intimately that even I lament their lost dignity and wildness. But then I remind myself: that dignity trip is my baggage, not theirs. They just want to survive, to reproduce, to flourish.

Despite Jen Beck's work at Crater Lake and similar efforts throughout the range of the whitebark pine, this twisted symbol of survival may not survive. Among other challenges, the warmer, wetter conditions we've created favor mountain hemlock and other densely clustered trees, which are now crowding out the whitebarks. Beck and her staff have gone out and girdled some of these interlopers in her planting sites, killing them with the same mechanism by which the bark beetle lays low its victims. "What is the point of having these resistant trees if the mountain hemlock are just going to smother them?" she asks.

Perhaps, through trying, through intervening, through planting rust-resistant seedlings (and in a few other places, not planting them), we'll learn more and become more effective at "managing" Earth. And that increased ability to consciously control, rather than just blunderingly influence, may well be distasteful to many. They would rather be mere passengers on Earth, taking our place among the other animals, living as part of an ecosystem but not as its master. Well, me too. That sounds less stressful, more pleasant. But that would mean abdicating our responsibility to the many species and ecosystems we've harmed with our lack of mastery. We owe it to them to improve our scientific understanding, our gardening prowess, so that we can ensure their continued persistence into the future.

Call it stewardship, call it gardening, call it what you will. It is our job—one I hope we can do together, democratically, with joy. And it is more important than being alone on the mountaintop or seeing the condor soar above us or even preserving the autonomy of wild places. All of that represents our relationship with the rest of nature. To be truly humble is to put other species first, and our relationship with them second.

Beck and I both have small children, and as we stand in the icy wind of the ridge, looking at the old trees that are dying and the baby seedling tops barely poking out of the snow, we are keenly aware that even if her work succeeds, the only thing our children will see here as adults will be a stand of small pines in callow youth, not yet carved by time and adversity into their beautiful maturity. But it's also possible that climate change and disease could sweep the whole park—the whole continent—clean of whitebarks old and young, and with them the bird that disperses their seeds, and maybe the small mammals and grizzly bears that eat those seeds. "The loss of a whole species is much greater than whatever wildness is lost from this action," Beck says. "This is humans trying to do the right thing."

LESLIE HARRISON

[Parable]

I wake and once again the trees have come the trees
have once again grown through me in sleep a tiny forest
tiny tangled copse come to populate all the windswept
all the empty spaces dendritic roots curl around cells
as if around stones and the furling tender leaves their
hungry wait for light and now the trees fill with birds
whose wings I feel as faint capillary flutter whose songs
rustle in the blood autumn now and the leaves loosen
begin their fall the tiny spiders move in set about their
careful work stitching leaves back to branches mending
the quilted sky the geese travel over and in the woods
the mist descends everything is indistinct bleached and
pale the mist tastes in the muscles the throat like a chill
when the mist dissipates it takes everything with it
branches leaves spiders their sticky useless sutures
even the trees are gone the spaces full of snow and now
the snow too is gone the spaces are meadows again
are empty again and now this is who is what I am

PLUM

GERONIMO G. TAGATAC

The Orchard

EFORE SUNRISE Saturday morning, my father laid two pairs of long-handled pruning shears and two curved saws in the trunk of our 1951 Pontiac. Then he put the cardboard box with the pots of food he'd cooked the night before—rice, adobo, and pinakbet—onto the floor of the back of the car. We drove south from San Jose until we came to Morgan Hill. I was silent during the trip.

It was my last year in high school and I wanted to spend Saturdays hanging out with my friends Terry, Robert, and Curt, to sit in the passenger seat of the blue, secondhand Mercury that Curt's father had bought him, cruising south on Highway 17, toward Santa Cruz, with the windows open and the radio playing Chuck Berry. I yearned to be on the boardwalk, listening to the rushing sound of the roller coaster and the girls screaming. I wanted to cruise down First Street with the guys, looking for reckless girls in hot cars. I dreamed of meeting a girl with thick, silky hair at a drive-in restaurant. I used to imagine the way she would look straight into my eyes as we talked, though I didn't exactly know what we'd talk about. Instead, I was going to be pruning trees.

We turned off Highway 101 onto a two-lane blacktop, and drove west for about five miles until we came to a gravel road that ran along the foot of a wooded hill, and drove some more. We turned up a dirt road and my father shifted into first gear. The car climbed up the rutted, narrow road toward the top of a ridge. What the hell could anybody be growing up there, I wondered. What are we going to prune, poison oak?

I didn't like what I saw when we got to the end of the road. It looked as though someone had thrown the orchard over the top of the ridge like a blanket. There wasn't a level patch of ground anywhere. I knew from experience that it would be a nightmare trying to keep our ladders from falling over, leaving us hanging on for dear life from a limb, or toppling off our ladders and killing ourselves. It was a prune orchard. Prune trees had so many small branches that it took forever to finish one. They were the worst thing possible when you were getting paid by the tree. Might as well be poison oak, I thought. My father didn't say anything.

A woman came out of the unpainted shack that stood at the end of the dirt road. She was a thin, dry stick of a woman. The oldest person I'd ever seen. She wore a black, longsleeved cotton dress that reached the ground. Her hair was covered with a black scarf knotted at the back of her neck. She had a hard-looking, tanned face with deep lines that ran around the edges of her mouth and faded, blue eyes. We'd be lucky to get fifty cents a tree out of this old bag.

"I'm Jacinto and this is my son, Missus." My father took off his brown felt work hat. "You talked to Mariano about us pruning your orchard." The old lady nodded, walked us over to a storage shed, and pointed to some ladders leaning against the side of it.

They were tall ladders, twelve-footers, so old that the wood had turned gray. Probably as ancient as the old crow. Some of the rungs had been replaced. Others had been strengthened with baling wire that ran under the rungs and was anchored rightly around the uprights. They were three feet wide at their bottoms, tapering to about a foot across at their tops. I chose one of the better-looking ones. I put my right arm between the rungs just below the ladder's middle, making sure that the hinged third leg was away from me. When I lifted, I heard it creak as it came away from the wall. I let the top of the ladder drop toward the ground in front of me, carrying it parallel to the ground, balanced like the arm of a scale on my shoulder, my arm pinning its outside leg against the ladder. I strode off toward the first row of waiting trees, leaving my father to talk price with the old woman.

When I got to the first tree of my row, I swung the ladder upright, throwing the long, hinged leg away from the ladder's body, setting it down, moving it again toward the tree's interior, leveling the ladder. I made a few more adjustments, so that its top was between the limbs I wanted to prune. I didn't want to move it any more than I had to. My father walked up carrying his own ladder and both pairs of shears.

"How much a tree?" I asked.

"Thirty-five cents."

"Thirty-five!"

"She can't afford more." He swung his ladder upright and threw its leg out. He got his level the first time, its top perfectly placed between two of his first tree's large limbs.

Thirty-five cents a tree and the damned trees were thick with new growth. They should have been pruned a month earlier and it was going to take a lot more work than usual to trim them. The more I thought about it, the angrier I got. But I knew it was useless to argue with my father. He was a just-off-the-boat Filipino. A penny-pinching Ilocano. He'd work himself to death for a dime a tree.

Sometime after three that afternoon, when I had finished my eighth tree, I climbed down from my ladder and was about to move it when I saw the old woman standing a few yards away, among the tangle of branches we had cut from her trees. She must have walked up between our rows, silently looking over our work, making sure we weren't butchering her orchard. She stood as still as the warm afternoon air, her dress hanging motionless, her face as hard as bark, her blue, shrewd eyes watchful. Not a leaf moved in the tree above her. I heard my father's shears stop, and when I looked up at him, he was tipping his hat to her from where he stood, high among the limbs. "Good afternoon, Missus," he said. And I, trying to keep my face from showing my anger, thought, You expect a hell of a lot for thirty-five cents a tree. She looked at my father and nodded without smiling, and then into my eyes. She must have sensed my resentment. Then she turned and walked back down the row toward her shack.

As I worked through the afternoon, I tried to cool the anger that filled my head and chest by thinking about the clothes that the money I earned would buy. I imagined the new cloth smell of the shirts and pants in their neat, colorful stacks on the shelves of the downtown Penney's department store. I remembered a thin black belt with a fancy imitation silver buckle, one that would go perfectly with my charcoal-colored, pleated wool slacks. I thought about leaving home and going away to state college. I'd get an office job, wear suits, and never go near another ladder.

I reached up with my shears to cut a thick sapling. The blade went a third of the way through and stopped. Fucking thing, I thought, straining at the handles. I tried cutting at another angle but it didn't work. Sweat was running into my eyes. I put all my strength into the handles, feeling the muscles in my chest and shoulders strain, watching the handles bow slightly. The blade cut another quarter inch and stopped. In a fury, I backed the blade out of the cut and tried to slam handles closed. My mind went red, then black. There was a loud snap and the resistance in the handles vanished. Got you, you son of a bitch! I said.

But when I looked at my shears, I realized that I had broken the right handle off at the lip of its metal socket. The shears and the left handle hung by the embedded blade, like some strange, wood-eating bird that had died in mid-bite. I stood silently among the crowded limbs and all sorts of thoughts went through me. That I was strong enough to break the hickory-handled shaft. That I was stronger than my father. That I wouldn't have to work for the rest of the day.

I looked over and saw my father watching me from across the space that separated us. His eyes went from my broken, dangling shears to my face and stayed there. I was overtaken by shame, and then, as I descended my ladder, I thought about the last time he'd lost his temper with me. I remembered the quick strides that had brought him suddenly within arm's reach and the way he had spun me around and hit me across the back, one, two, three times, with his strong right hand. But this time he walked up to me, reached out, took both pieces of the shears from my hands, and looked at them sadly. Then he said, "What's the matter with you? Now I have to work the rest of the day to buy a new pair. Get away from me before you make me mad. Go on, get away from me." Then he turned, walked over to his ladder, put the broken shears onto the ground, and went back into his tree.

I went as far away from my father as I could go without leaving the orchard. I sat down at the orchard's edge, with my back against a tree, looking out at the scrub oak and madrone. I listened to the distant sound of my father's shears and the rasp of his saw, all through the hot afternoon. When the sun reached the ridge to the west and the light was going from yellow to orange, I heard the sound of his voice calling me to him. It was a distant, familiar sound that came out of the darkening rows of trees. The same voice that had sometimes called me in from play in the summers of my childhood. I walked over to where he waited by the car. We did not speak all the way home and we did not go to work in the orchard on the next day, which was Sunday.

We returned to the old lady's orchard the following Saturday morning, a week later. When we got there, my father reached into the open car trunk and handed me my shears. One new, lighter handle contrasted sharply with its dark, worn mate and the oiled, gray metal blade. I remember thinking that he must have had to do a lot of searching to find a place that stocked a pruning shear handle. I'd never seen one in any of the hardware stores. He had painstakingly removed the broken piece of wood shaft from its socket, replacing it with a new one. As I took the shears from him, he laughed very softly. In the early morning air, that laughter came to me as a sign that his anger was gone. Then he said, "Take it easy on these, Superman."

We worked through the morning, the silence broken only by the snap of our shears going through slim new limbs, the "suckers." Once I heard an airliner pass high overhead, leaving a single white seam that divided the empty blue sky. I stood on my ladder and looked up through the tree's almond-shaped leaves at the vapor trail and dreamed of flying through the clean cold air.

The old woman came out to inspect our work at midmorning, walking along the rows we'd finished like a dark shadow. She nodded up at both of us and seemed pleased.

Moving my ladder, I paused to watch my father work. He wasted no motion, never seemed to hurry. Yet he always outdistanced me when we were pruning. I'd watched him work at that unceasing pace since my childhood, when I was old enough to walk out to the edge of a lettuce field he was thinning.

"What you going to do with all the money you make?" He called down to me from his ladder.

"I'm going to rent a tuxedo for the senior prom."

"You better save your money for college."

"I've already invited someone."

"Tell her you can't go."

"I can't do that. She's already bought a dress. Besides, everyone goes to their senior prom."

"Okay, but you're wasting money you're going to need next year."

He wound up lending me the money to rent a tuxedo. "You can pay me back later. Save your money for school," he said.

On the afternoon that I brought the tuxedo home from the rental shop, I laid the whole thing out on my bed. I had never seen anything like the starched white shirt with its generous French cuffs, or the gleaming patent-leather pumps. My father came into my room and stood beside me. He ran his hands over the satin, drop-shroud collar of the dinner jacket that lay on my bed. Almost without thinking, I asked, "Would you like to try it on?"

He looked into my eyes and smiled suddenly. Then he took off his shirt. The starched sleeve of the dress shirt made a tearing sound as it separated to receive his muscled brown arm. I helped him with the shirt studs and cuff links. Then he slipped on the black slacks with their shiny, satin stripes. When he'd put on the bow tie, the cummerbund, and the pumps, I held the dinner jacket out for him as he slid his left, then his right arm into their silk-lined sleeves. I followed him out of my room, to the full-length mirror at the end of the hall, and watched him stand before it for a few moments. He put his hands in the pockets of the slacks and turned so that he was in profile. At that moment, he looked as though he were standing casually on an early evening corner of a big city street, waiting for a cab to take him to some downtown nightclub. It felt good to see him smile.

Then he said, "Let me show you something."

He went into his and my mother's bedroom and, after a few minutes, he brought out a shoe box, which he took into the kitchen. He put the box on the kitchen table, poured us each a cup of coffee, and when we had sat down beside each other, he opened the box and took out a small pile of photographs.

I looked at the old, black-and-white photos and I saw him as a young man, two years in this country. There was one picture of him standing with his Filipino friends. They were serious-looking young men in crisp, white shirts and ties swirling with bold patterns and colors I could only guess at. They wore suits with double-breasted jackets that tapered in at the waists, accentuating their narrow hips.

I looked down at my father's unlined face and realized that none of them could have been more than twenty years old. Their eyes were the strong, sure, dark eyes of those who had crossed thousands of miles between two worlds and survived. They were men who had all of their dreams before them. They stood very straight and their eyes looked across thirty years at me, saying, Look at us. Remember us.

The following Saturday I came up with a good row. It had lots of small trees. I was able to keep pace with my father and even pull ahead of him for a while. When he saw my luck, he laughed and said, "Think you can keep up with the old man?" In the middle of the afternoon, when I had pruned my way through the small trees and come upon one thick with new growth, he overtook me. I was glad for his company. I think that he must have known this because he did not pass me but kept pace with me for what remained of the day.

He told me a story about the time when, as a boy in his family's hamlet, in the Philippines, he'd stolen bananas from his Uncle Claro's tree. He'd taken so many of the ripe fruit that he had to hide a few under each of his mother's clay jars. My father said he'd hidden in some bushes and watched his mother's astonishment as she turned over jar after jar and kept finding bananas.

Then my father laughed. And his laughter was a soft, insistent sound that rose from a coughlike whisper to a strong, full-voiced sound that filled the space around us, infecting me with the vision of his mother's astonishment. And I laughed with him. I remember our laughter and the sound of the cut limbs falling to the ground beneath us like some very slow, heavy rain.

One afternoon, at the end of our eighth Saturday in the orchard, I stepped off the bottom rung of my ladder and realized we had pruned all the trees. There was nothing to do but gather the

cuttings into small piles for burning, then to stack our ladders
against the shed for the last time.

We walked through the orchard to the old woman's shack, to
where she waited on the front porch. She had brought out a bottle
of red wine and a glass for my father. For me she had opened a
bottle of orange soda. She filled the glass with wine and handed
it to my father, then invited us to sit on the front steps. My father,
who almost never drank, raised his glass to her, said, "Thank you,
Missus," and sipped her wine. I did the same, in unison with my
father, smiling at her. She smiled back and said, "You and your
son good workers. You do good job." Hearing her speak for the
first time, I could not place her accent. When my father finished
his wine, she offered him more, but he refused politely. Then he
handed her a scrap of paper on which he had written in pencil the
number of trees we had pruned, the amount per tree, and the total.
She took the paper into the shack. In a few minutes, she returned
with a handful of bills and some change.

"You count," she said, handing the money to my father. He
handed her back a ten. "Too much."

She refused to take it. "For the boy."

"No, no, Missus." He tried to hand the money to her. But she
put her hands behind her back and would not take the money. He
tried again. Again, she refused. Finally, he folded the bills, put them
into his shirt pocket, and thanked her.

The old woman stood on her porch and watched us go back
through her orchard, the way we had come on the first day. I
walked beside my father, carrying the shears with the mismatched
handles. Once I looked back at her and waved. And as we walked,
I saw, as I had seen in other orchards, how the unburdened limbs

of the trees made them seem cleaner and lighter, as though we had helped them to shed some of their years.

We put our shears and saws into the car. Then my father went off by himself between two rows of trees, looking up at their tops, sometimes stooping to pick up a stray twig, tossing it onto one of the brush piles. I watched him walk over the ground that bore the marks of our boots and ladders. He went all the way down the row until, in the fading light, I could no longer distinguish the khaki color of his work pants from his faded blue work shirt, or the dark brown color of his old, felt work hat from his black hair. I watched him grow smaller and smaller, until I nearly lost sight of him in the thickness of the distant trees.

Then one cloudy September morning, my father drove me downtown, to the Greyhound station where I was to catch a bus north to start my first semester of college. I was wearing the clothes that I'd bought with my pruning money: cotton pants, white shirt with a button-down collar, and a blue V-neck sweater. My father stood with me as I waited to board my bus and, just before I got into the line of people who were giving their tickets to the bus driver, my father took my hand in both of his own dark, calloused hands. "Call me when you get there. It's all right to call collect." He looked into my eyes for a moment and smiled. "You run out of money, you can come back and prune trees with me." Then he released my hand, turned, and walked across the station's cool tiled floor. I watched him until he disappeared through the glass and metal-framed front doors of the station. Then I got into line, handed my ticket to the driver, and climbed into the bus.

As the driver swung the bus out of the station, I watched the brick-fronted buildings slide by. I tried to imagine what the coming weeks would be like—college, a new town, the books waiting to be read. It began to rain as the bus went past the park where the tall oaks reached up through the heavy streaks of rain. I was thinking of the old woman's prune orchard where I had stood on my ladder among the pale green leaves. The bus pulled onto the freeway and, as I sat alone with the rising sound of the engine, I knew I would never see the old woman again. And then I remembered the sound of my father's laughter filling the air between the trees.

LUCIA MARIA PERILLO

Maypole

The tanagers have returned to my dead plum tree—
they sip the pond through narrow beaks.
Orange and yellow, this recurrence
that comes with each year's baby leaves.

And if the tree is a church and spring is Sunday,
the birds are fancy hats of women breaking into song
Or say the tree is an old car whose tank is full,
then the birds are girls on a joy ride
crammed in its seats. Or if the tree is the carnival
lighting the tarmac of the abandoned mall by the freeway
then the birds are the men with pocketknives
who erect its Ferris wheel.

Or say the tree is the boat that chugs into port
to fill its hold and deck with logs,
then the birds are the Russian sailors who
rise in the morning in the streets where they've slept,
rubbing their heads and muttering
these beautiful words that no one understands.

MAGNOLIA

LIA PURPURA

On Photographing Children in Trees

A meditation

THE PROS ARE OUT with their props and equipment—wipes for the sap and the acorn stains, noisemaking toys and funny balloons, so eyes up and look here!—that it might seem the kids aren't arranged, the trees not decorative, and a girl is called out of real reverie, a tree-climbing haze, to be photographed for a holiday card then released. As if the light around the trees were not amped by big reflective screens, and the trees did not mind posing as Nature, garland, or frame. Such is the dream of pastoral time, free and unmanaged here in the park, preserved by a child in the fat crown of an oak, still green, no gold roughing in, no falling yet, it isn't fall yet, just very high summer suspended.

It looks like that tree might be *her* tree—where she goes to hear

herself speak, tree demanding no words, but tender in the space
between nose and bark (scent of pond water, cinnamon, musk)—
where ants on their village roads haul their bundles, their burdens,
intentions, in strict, ordered lines. From where I'm standing, I
can see her trying—how to admit those whose voices and bodies
disrupt the clear ant-thoughts that touch her deep in and call her to
breathe a warm safety-cloud over their fear.

The trees of my childhood? Both yardbound and wild, holding
their street corners, shadows, birdsong. A mimosa, whose pinfeather
blossoms grew into explosions that held on for weeks, then unpinked
and puddled up brown in the driveway—and the double-take, heart-
slash when just recently I heard it called a *trash tree*—as strange and
world-tilting as learning someone you loved and thought funny,
irreverent, so fully alive (as maybe you'd be if lucky, when grown)
was *a drunk* at all those parties. And still you keep on with your love's
bright refusals. The crab apple: my father cut a branch after it split
in a storm and made my mother a cane from it, bowed in the center
like a leg with rickets, but she loved it and refused the upright steel
one. The fishing tree—what my son called the dogwood where he
and my father played their games, and which for me early on could
be petted, called to, and fed. And central in my grandmother's patch
of backyard, the white birch, its cool skin so pink and damp when
I laid my hand on it, whose job it was to shade the devotionals, her
tomatoes and roses, prizewinning if she'd been after prizes, lavished
with care, tended in the small space available here in the New World.
I was no immigrant, but the birch and I spoke like a couple who,
from different countries, used a third language between them.

It has always been so on holiday cards: backlit child on swing
at sunset; or at the shore, poking a starfish with a shy finger, or

handed a flower to sniff for innocence—or as it is today, just across
from the park, a sister and brother in matching white shirts, posed
on a bench on a rolling green lawn with arms cued around each
other's shoulders, meaning love (more a respite from fighting if
you'd seen them before they were yelled at). Four times a year, on
the white-shirted kids' lawn, up go the yellow warning flags, with
person and dog figures X'd out and a date written in when it'll be
safe again to play, the poison absorbed and the excess washed off
into the bay. Before the family moved in last year, ivy tangled up the
stone walls and darkened the mossy root folds of old maples. At the
edge of their property was a tremendous magnolia, an extravagance
I'd cross three neighborhoods to see. It was crawl-space private
underneath and smelled of iron-mud-worms. Its blooms were
made of milk and blood, fire and cream. After a few weeks they tore
out everything green, cut down the magnolia, and rolled lengths
of sod over the graded yard and around the stump like a bunched,
bulky scarf. The cut tree sent out buds, then shoots, came partly
back as a magnolia bush, and maybe would've been more, but a
stump grinder finished it off.

All this for a lawn where no kids play but get propped and cajoled,
instructed in poise, which means to please, to be pleasing—which
is someone else's need, not yours and you'll have to fight that too,
dear girl in a tree refusing to look at the camera and smile, you
who'd rather go dark, hands cupped like horse blinders, face in the
bark so one single ray at a time is admitted and shines on the sap
where a stuck ant part meets you deep in, where something's now
blowing across the lake of my chest, loosening my ribs, all my parts
slipping and I'm no more-than, just bigger-than ant, very softened
beneath my skin, light sharp on that bit of ant body (and I'm sorry,

always—why sorry? For seeing?), while the whole and intact ants
file over the rough bark, so when I look up inside my head where
the colors come and snap and burst, the parts that are broken ride
themselves back into the black night's full body.

WESTERN RED CEDAR

Terese Mailhot

The Dominion of Roots

Gifts of the cedar

HAVE YOU EVER given your whole body to a people? There are people who know the paradise of my affection   whose mothers smell like clay. People who remember me. I won't be taken down for Prospect Park, for new roads and homes. I am a home to them.

In my knotted side, I know virus and antidote, club and bowl— destruction and restitution. We know the power of a lightning bolt enough to revere it, to pray to it, and sometimes, to pray for it.

What my people know of me is that I listen. It's enough some- times—to listen. I hold the story of the first fire. I hold every gener- ation of women, every matriarch and healer. My apex reaches beyond the fog each morning, and I can see their small lives, chim- neys and smoke. I can see, sometimes, children who are as much a testimony to survival as me.

I don't want to know this floodplain barren. My people know when I go—we go—it's why the women hand-drum *Remember me, remember me.*

I can say forever and mean it. I can hold a woman above and beneath me. The seed of me belongs to the woman who planted it, who put me in the ground, encircled by women who came before her, who are seeded to roots that stretch toward me.

The women and I know vanishment—what it's like to be untethered and unburied. There are many wrong ways to die. The right way to live, in this world, is to be rooted here. I never want to leave. I want so desperately to stay in soundless being, watching over the people. I'd like to know my own decay and to be revived again, untouched by the ways of white men.

The women wish that too. The women need that too. Forever is a foreign land to everything but trees. What can't you know in the dominion of roots? What can't a woman do, restored by me?

In a deep grief, a woman weaves a crown of harvested root for her own head. A woman weaves a basket and paints herself red. A woman puts down her tobacco and tells a story at my base like a conjuring and asks me for strength.

I can give it. I speak in stillness.

The woman can't let go, like me. She's tired and hollow, sinking into the undertow of something beyond me. She knows instinctively to touch the earth, and strength rises out and in like life does, and between us, every visit is a blessing. A woman knows surging power.

Relationality is to give grace that crosses one body to another. What is it like to be born from grace and to die beneath it, memorialized in canoe and river, spirit and song. I want to be a paddle that sinks soft and rhythmic in the water.

To vanish the grief of a young death in her community, a woman breaks down the bad medicine of white monuments and tells her daughter that warriors don't fight as much as they are willing to die for some things.

"You know?" She points at me as if I'm a religion—a culture— good medicine worth fighting for.

The daughter nods and plants sticky fingers on me.

"If they tell you you're nothing, don't listen."

The girl nods again.

They plant a new sister. The woman tells her daughter, "If you ever feel weak, come here. Touch the ground."

It's in the girl to think she'll never need to. In time, she'll be here. She'll make a practice of remembering, as her mother did before her.

Now, though, it hurts her mother to hold her gaze—only a tree could understand the sorrow of time and history any deeper, her mother thinks. She couldn't mourn her mother until she became one. In every finger, wrapped around her index, she remembers a love that rests now in me.

The girl looks like her mother in thirty years. She takes a bough to smell its green. The women live so long beneath me and above. My perch is strange and all over like the best energies.

If I could give my body to a people in one generation, it would be enough, but eight generations of women have celebrated me and pared down my life and given me such clarity and mission, I don't know a body without a people to receive it.

And they say Jesus is a martyr. What of me? Restoring each day—sleeping each winter, waking up to harvest and flora and fractal life, and daughters who are red in the medicine wheel and their love is so far reaching I can barely contain my hope with each new lifting sun.

I belong to warriors. My rust on their sleeves. My bark on their backs. A grandmother boils cedar tea to fill the house, to clear every throat. The song that comes belongs to me. What fills the house is me. Each woman, a monument to root and quietude and all medicine. What does it mean to never die, to give my body to a people, and to receive so much?

What does it mean that the grandmother used to be a girl who kept cedar in her pillow at the boarding school? When they called her number, three, she stood at attention, scared for her body and future. It would be ten long years of that, and when she could walk in her own skin, with her own prayers, she came back to me. What would it mean, had I not been there to receive her? What kind of pain would that have been?

LILAH HEGNAUER

A Poet Friend Tells Me Nature Imagery Is Dead

What if it wasn't just an oak tree?
If there was a teacup on the big, low
branch and Allison hoisted me up
to sit and drink tea with my feathered

friend, is that dead? What if it wasn't
a robin sitting on the other side of my saucer,
chatting about the lower Cascades'
different shades of green? If the robin

was full of seed and swelled till he burst,
would you say the imagery matched
our violent culture? I'd like to see
the half-digested sunflower seeds

spewed on the branch, if for nothing more
than the textured gray upon brown.
Salmonberries hedge the footpath.
Allison eats them from the bush

and her fingers drip with the juice
of the labor of it. It's all been said.
We don't believe in love poetry.
But maybe it's not love poetry

(damn it) to say the oak existed,
one afternoon, while two women
picked berries and skipped work
and played out the odd two-step

of the long married and childless.
There was no tea, no robin; just her
hip flask of vodka, the finches and
sparrows, and a million shades of green.

NORWAY MAPLE

Michael Pollan

Trees as Metaphors

FROM MY DESK in my barn loft I have a good view of the new maple tree I planted, and whenever my attention wanders from my work, it seems to settle there, amid its leafless branches. A frail thing to burden with so much reflection, I know, but that seems to be the fate of trees in a world of humans—our thoughts and metaphors cling to them like iron filings to a magnet. Yet every time we think we've figured out what a tree *really* is—the habitation of gods, a commodity, part and parcel of transcendent nature, component of the forest ecosystem—it turns out we've simply come up with a temporarily handy new description of it. Still, our metaphors matter. Indeed, our metaphors about trees by and large determine the fate of trees.

My hunch is that we sense our old metaphors about trees, and nature as a whole, are wearing thin and we're casting around for new and more powerful ones. By the time my maple reaches its maturity, it probably will mean something very different from what it means today.

What might these new metaphors be? Some philosophers and activists have recently advanced the notion that my tree (and nature generally) possesses "rights." One legal scholar, Christopher D. Stone, has gone so far as to argue that forests, lakes, and mountains should be granted the right to sue (called "standing") in American courts.

I'm not sure I like the idea of my tree growing up to be litigious. Can't we come up with a metaphor less awkward than one based on "rights"? In fact, science has recently proposed some new descriptions of trees that strike me as much more promising, and that, in retrospect, lend mankind's old, strong feelings about trees an eerie prescience.

Think of the tree as Earth's breathing apparatus, an organ that helps regulate the planet's atmosphere by exhaling fresh oxygen and inhaling the carbon that animals, decay, and civilization spew into it. The tree, under this new description, is not merely a member of the local forest ecosystem (where we've known for some time that it exerts considerable influence on the local life, soil, and even climate); it's also a vital organ in a global system more intricate and interdependent than we ever realized. Earth may not be a spaceship but an organism, and trees may be its lungs.

Given the choice, I would much prefer to see the Lung Tree catch on than the Litigious Tree. The lung metaphor puts us in a reciprocal relation with trees once again. If we come to think of trees as lungs and Earth as an organism, it will no longer make sense to think of ourselves as being outside nature, or even to think of trees as being outside culture. Indeed, the whole inside/outside metaphor might wither away, and that would be a good thing.

It's obviously impossible to predict what new metaphors will catch on. I do know this, though: if I could have news of my maple one hundred years from now, I would know a great deal about nature's fate. One day not long ago, I gave some thought to exactly what sort of news of my tree I would want. Certainly a botanist's report on my tree's health would be useful. The Norway maple is a cool-weather species, and if it has sickened in the heat of 2091, I will know that the greenhouse effect was real and that we did not avert it. But perhaps more revealing than a scientist's account would be a letter from that time, one that happened to devote a few sentences of description to my tree, in everyday language. From that I might learn how people in 2091 looked at a tree, and this would pretty much tell me how nature was faring then. If the letter described the tree in terms that would have been familiar to us—or to Henry Thoreau, for that matter—that would be cause for worry, for it would mean we'd gotten mired in old metaphors about nature and had probably failed to extricate ourselves from our predicament.

But maybe the letter would bring evidence of a new metaphor, something vivid and powerful and, for a time at least, true. At first it would probably seem strange, even incomprehensible. But eventually its sense would dawn. *So that's what a tree is! How could we ever have thought otherwise?* There might then be reason to hope that some new truth had put down roots, that perhaps we had put our relationship to nature on a sounder footing at last.

REDWOOD

RICHARD PRESTON

A Day of Discovery

Seeking out the largest living things on Earth

THE RAINFOREST in Jedediah Smith Redwoods State Park is exceptionally dense—among the densest rainforests anywhere on Earth. The interior of the park is a warren of tiny, steep notch canyons and gullies. The forest understory consists of virtually impassable thickets of huckleberry bushes and salmonberry canes and ferns and small trees. The salmonberry canes are covered with prickles, which over hours of scraping can turn a person's exposed skin into an ooze of blood. Visibility in Jed Smith can be poor to near zero.

One day in early May 1998, Steve Sillett, a botanist and professor of redwood forest ecology at Humboldt State University, called Michael Taylor, a naturalist and longtime friend, and said, "Let's go out and try to find some champion trees." They decided to go to Jed Smith, a California state park along the Smith River, twenty miles south of the Oregon border. They were intrigued by a complex of small valleys that appears on the U.S. Geological Survey's topographic maps just to the south of Route 199, inside the park. No trails led into the valleys, and the terrain was a clog of redwood jungle.

An evergreen conifer and a member of the cypress family, the coast redwood grows in valleys and on mountains along the central . and northern coast of California, mostly within ten miles of the sea. It is the tallest species of tree on Earth. Its scientific name is *Sequoia sempervirens*. Sometimes it is called the California redwood, but most often it is simply referred to as the redwood.

About a month earlier, and about a mile and a half up one of the valleys, Taylor and Sillett had discovered a giant redwood that they named New Hope; they had given it this name because they felt that it gave them hope of finding more titans there. The oldest and most massive redwoods are called titans—not the tallest ones, but the biggest. Botanists make a distinction between the height of a tree and its overall size, which is measured by the volume of wood in the tree. The tallest redwoods are nearly 380 feet tall; titans are typically more than 300 feet tall, but they can contain four to five times more wood mass than the tallest redwoods. Redwood titans are among the largest individual living organisms in nature.

Now Taylor and Sillett planned to push deeper into Jed Smith, beyond New Hope Tree, to explore valleys where they had never gone before. It seemed unlikely that anyone had gone there in many years, and they would discover, once they got into the valleys, that the U.S. government maps of the area were inaccurate and could not be used for guidance. For all practical purposes, the center of Jed Smith was a blank spot on the map of North America.

They decided to make the trip on May 11. It was a Monday, and Taylor was supposed to work at RadioShack that day, but he called in sick. Sillett picked him up at his Arcata apartment early in the morning and they drove north. They didn't bring any food with them, or warm clothing, because they assumed that they would be home by afternoon. They also didn't bring a GPS locator device, because GPS devices typically don't work in redwood forests. They didn't bring cell phones, either, because cell phones also rarely work in redwood forests. They parked in a turnout along Route 199 and went into the forest, pushing southward and upward along a creek toward New Hope Tree.

For the first quarter mile, they had to crawl through underbrush on their hands and knees, sometimes lying flat on their stomachs and belly-crawling. They wormed under tight masses of huckleberry bushes, or they turned their bodies sideways and rammed through them. Taylor was holding a laser range finder—a device to estimate the heights of redwood trees—in one hand, trying to keep it from getting wet, and Sillett was carrying another in a knapsack.

After an hour and a half of clawing up the stream, they had gone about a mile. They regarded this as very rapid progress. They arrived at a fork in the creek, and both drainages headed up into notch valleys, one leading west, the other east. They followed the west fork. Sillett was wearing long sleeves, but Taylor was wearing only a T-shirt, and his arms began to bleed. The valley narrowed, blocked by fallen redwood trunks. They climbed over and around them, and arrived at New Hope Tree. It had taken them two hours to cover a mile and a half of known terrain. They rested underneath New Hope, drank some water, and consulted the map.

The map showed a knoll, or peak, about a mile above New Hope Tree, in the middle of a warren of tiny valleys. They decided to make their objective the peak, where they might get a view, and then turn around and go home.

They began pushing into unknown terrain. Two hours later, they had gone just three-quarters of a mile farther up the gorge, which opened into a basin full of Douglas firs mixed with redwoods. It was getting on toward noon. Both of them were tired and hungry, Taylor particularly so. He weighed 220 pounds, and his knees were beginning to hurt. They stopped and debated whether to turn back, then consulted the map. The USGS topographic map showed the knoll right where they were. But there was no peak. Instead of a peak, the land went down and formed a basin.

USGS topographic maps are constructed by means of aerial photographs. In some cases, the area is not also surveyed on the ground. It would be exceedingly difficult to survey the terrain in Jed Smith, because visibility in the forest is exceptionally poor. Aerial photographs can reveal the shape of the top surface of the canopy, but they can't reveal the underlying terrain. In a redwood forest, the landforms can differ dramatically from the shape of the top of the canopy.

In his explorations of other forests, Taylor had often seen small marks on redwoods—cuts in the bark, splashes of faded paint—that had been left by timber cruisers, men looking for trees to cut. Timber cruisers were early explorers of the redwood forest (after the Native Americans), and they went through the forests mostly during the twentieth century. Timber cruisers' marks persist for more than a hundred years, but this basin, Taylor noticed, had no timber-cruiser marks on the trees. "I honestly don't think any people had been in that place in a very long time," he said to me.

"I sometimes wonder if people had been in there at any time after the discovery of the New World by Europeans."

Taylor and Sillett put their map away, because it wasn't doing them any good, and crossed the basin in search of higher ground. Some two hours later, they reached the edge of the basin. They wanted to turn around and go back the way they had come, but they saw no landmarks, the map was useless, and they didn't know exactly where they were. Instead, they went upslope, deeper into the center of the park. "We need to find an exit creek that will take us out of here," Sillett said to Taylor.

They began crossing a rugged, up-and-down plateau clad with rainforest. It dropped down into another small basin that didn't appear on the map, and they came to a saddle between two ridges. Now afternoon, they had been going for seven hours. They began to zigzag back and forth, trying to find some feature of the land that was on the map.

Michael Taylor was beginning to get scared. Steve Sillett was in better physical condition than Taylor was. The air temperature was in the fifties, and he was wearing only his cotton T-shirt. If it got dark and began to rain, the temperature could drop into the forties and they would be soaked. In that kind of weather, a person wearing wet cotton clothing can get hypothermia, which is a very serious matter. They were seven hours of hard bushwhacking from any sort of help—but they didn't know exactly in which directions to go. They hadn't eaten in many hours, yet they had burned up large amounts of energy moving through the underbrush.

Sillett became worried about Taylor. He noticed that Taylor had a crazy and potentially dangerous way of moving through redwood jungle. When he came to a big redwood log, he would climb up

onto it and sit there, and then he would fall off the log, disappear-
ing on the far side with a crash. "You're going to break your leg," he
told Taylor, and Taylor answered that you have to let your body go
limp as you fall, and then you won't break anything. Sillett called
the move the Taylor Flop. Even though Taylor was in worse shape
physically, he kept moving ahead of Sillett, flopping and crashing
over logs. He seemed unstoppable.

They arrived at a waterless gully, a slot chasm choked with
underbrush and blanketed in forest. They pushed down into the
slot and came to a huge Douglas fir. When they measured the tree
with their lasers and a tape line, they discovered that it was the largest Douglas fir in California. They named it Ol' Jed. The discovery
lifted their spirits momentarily.

The chasm continued downward beyond the tree, and they kept
following it, hoping that it would come out somewhere, but it was
a trap. They were mostly crawling through bushes, or sliding over
boulders, or climbing over piles of huge redwood logs. The gully
didn't seem to be going anywhere useful. "I suggest we call it Ruthlor Gulch," Sillett said to Taylor. "This describes its ruthless and
unforgiving nature."

An hour into Ruthlor Gulch, Taylor, whose knees were beginning to swell up, sat down and refused to go any farther. "We
should go back," he said. "None of this matches what's on the
map. I don't want to have to sleep underneath a log." They hadn't
brought a flashlight.

"We'll never find our way back," Sillett said.

"I'm turning back anyway."

"Dude! We can't turn back. We're committed to a heinous
bushwhack."

At this point, Taylor blew up. He called Sillett a fucking tree fanatic. Sillett told him to speak for himself. They began yelling at each other.

Eventually, they calmed down and agreed that they had better behave like gentlemen or they were truly going to be hosed. "Look, we have to come out somewhere," Sillett said.

They didn't. Ruthlor Gulch just went on and on, for three hours. During that time they covered about a mile. It was a mile of worming, crawling, bleeding, sliding, Taylor-flopping, and cursing. Taylor began to have more difficulty walking as his swollen knees became more painful. Finally, the gulch came out into a nameless creek jammed with boulders and logs, flowing in an uncertain direction. They began to crawl in the water, because the creek was too choked with brush to stand up in.

An hour later, they were still crawling in the creek. They began referring to it as Cocksmoker Creek. The sun began to set, and the air became chilled. They were soaked. Taylor got the shakes from exposure to the cold water. It was apparent that a cold night was coming on. They weren't carrying any matches. Sillett and Taylor had decided long ago that they would never light a fire in a redwood forest under any circumstances.

Taylor, who was leading the way, came to a fallen redwood trunk that bridged the creek. When he climbed onto it and stood up, he saw that the creek had come out onto level ground. Directly in front of him was a curving wall of wood that blocked his view. It was the largest redwood that blocked his view. It was the largest redwood trunk he had seen in all his years of exploring the North Coast.

"*Aieeeee!*" he screamed.

Sillett wondered if Taylor had finally broken his leg, but then he saw the titan. They circled around it. It turned out to be, in fact, two monumental redwoods joined at the base—a twin tree—with a combined diameter of thirty feet. It has since been named the Screaming Titans by Steve Sillett.

They thought they had made a fine discovery, but the discovery had just begun. When they walked past the twin titans, they emerged into a grassy glade. Patches of open sky were visible, and pools of water shimmered. Around the edges of the glade stood a ring-shaped colonnade of undiscovered redwood titans.

The hair was standing up on the back of Taylor's neck. He and Sillett didn't know what to say to each other. They felt as if they had walked into a dream. The stars were beginning to come out, and Venus was up. The trees were outlined against a deep-blue dusk. Near the Screaming Titans they encountered two monstrous redwoods, which Sillett would later name Eärendil and Elwing. They waded through the pools of water and approached the row of titans growing on the far side of the colonnade. They ran Taylor's measuring tape around the nearest one. It proved to be one of the largest redwoods ever to have been found; they would name it El Viejo del Norte (The Old Man of the North). Next to it grows a redwood that they named the Lost Monarch.

In 2003, Sillett completed a scientific mapping project of the Lost Monarch and found that it was the largest living redwood in the world. The Lost Monarch contains at least forty thousand cubic feet of wood. Its trunk is thirty feet across near the base—wider than the General Sherman, the giant sequoia in the Sierra Nevada that is the world's largest tree in terms of volume and mass. The General Sherman is bigger than the Lost Monarch because its trunk has a cylindrical shape, like a stovepipe, while the Lost Monarch's trunk tapers slightly as it rises.

A redwood titan that was later given the name Stalagmight grows near the Lost Monarch, and there is Aragorn, Sacajawea, and Aldebaran. There are others. They are, collectively, the largest redwood trees on the planet.

The Grove of Titans exists at the bottom of a hidden, notchlike valley deep in Jedediah Smith Redwoods State Park. It was previously unknown to park officials and biologists. The trees in the grove had undoubtedly been looked at over the years by occasional bushwhackers or earlier timber cruisers looking for trees to cut, but nobody had understood how enormous they are. The Park Service surveyed and constructed a number of trails inside Jed Smith during the 1930s, but none of the trails entered the Grove of Titans.

As he walked through the grove for the first time, Taylor began crying.

The date of Taylor and Sillett's discovery of the Grove of Titans— May 11, 1998—is known to some botanists as the Day of Discovery.

When biologists visit the grove today, they vary their approach paths, so that their footsteps won't create a visible trail on the forest floor. The exact location of the grove is known only to a handful of biologists who climb the trees and study the ecology of the grove. They guard the knowledge of its location with the jealousy of a prospector who has found a mother lode.

Officially, the "largest" redwood in Jedediah Smith State Park has been the Stout Tree, which grows in the center of the Stout Grove, near the Smith River, close to a road and a parking lot. On weekends in summer, dozens of people can be seen walking around the Stout Tree, looking at it and taking pictures of it.

"The Stout Tree isn't even among the top fifty largest redwoods at Jed Smith," Michael Taylor once said to me.

He and Sillett eventually did get out of the woods that day, and they bummed a ride from a man they found photographing the Stout Tree. He kindly drove them back to their car. At nine o'clock at night on the Day of Discovery, they were stuffing themselves with cheeseburgers at Carl's Jr. in Crescent City. As he wolfed down his second double cheeseburger, it occurred to Taylor that he was eating too much. When he finished his dinner, he made a vow to honor the discovery of the Grove of Titans by going on a diet. Taylor soon lost fifteen pounds, and became a trim, fit man with well-developed muscles and no visible fat. In addition to being possibly the leading discoverer of giant trees in the history of botany, Michael Taylor is also the discoverer of the Taylor Diet. "It's simple," he explained to me. "I realized I was eating a lot. So I stopped eating a lot."

Robert Van Pelt, a scientist who had been climbing and studying trees with Steve Sillett, is in his own right one of the leading discoverers of giant trees. He is the author of *Forest Giants of the Pacific Coast,* a book that describes some of the largest known trees of various species, including redwoods. One day I was driving along the California Coast Highway with Van Pelt—we were going to look at some redwoods together—and he said, in an offhand way, "In the history of botany in the twentieth century, there was never a day like the Day of Discovery, and there will never be a day like it again."

"Why is that?" I asked.

"Because there is nothing on Earth like those trees left to be found," he said.

ADRIAN MATEJKA

It's Impossible to Breathe Trees

The whole snowy carapace rustles as trees
bend in needful poses & the knuckled trucks
pass below them again crunching road salt.
& we can all be thankful that the mittened
hands & knitted hats & lingering Christmases
with real presents under pretend trees can't
stop the thick thaw from happening in the next
couple of months. All of the buds cracking
open at the first unsealing of somebody's
winterized windows. The piano music
the windows used to muffle keying easily.
A cough of rabbits, then a stretch of birds—
little victories in the sky. Buttercup blossoms
breaking at shoe height & my little girl:
constant swirl of splendor. It will be good
to run through the tight curls of bees
as the trees share their ideas just beneath us.
It will be good to watch everything spin
effortlessly, as if we weren't even here.

FLORIDA TORREYA

MICHELLE NIJHUIS

To Take Wilderness in Hand

While scientists debate how to help save species from a
warming climate, others aren't willing to wait

ORREYA STATE PARK perches on the steep, sandy banks of the Apalachicola, where the river twists slowly through the Florida Panhandle toward the Gulf of Mexico. This is one of the most isolated spots in Florida, rich only in plant life and prisons, stupefyingly hot in summer and eerily quiet nearly all year-round. Most park visitors are on their way somewhere else, and when Connie Barlow stopped here on a winter day in 1999, she was no exception.

Barlow, trim and now in her fifties, is a writer and naturalist with cropped hair and a childlike air of enthusiasm. She's given to wandering, and back then she shuttled between a trailer in southern New Mexico and an apartment in New York City. That winter, during a detour to Florida, she paused at the park for a look at its raison d'être—an ancient tree species called *Torreya taxifolia*, familiarly known as the Florida torreya or, less romantically, stinking cedar. The park lies at the heart of the tree's tiny range, which stretches little more than twenty miles from the Georgia state line toward the mouth of the Apalachicola. But even at Torreya State Park, Barlow discovered, the Florida torreya is hard to find.

Torreya taxifolia was once a common sight along the Apalachicola, plentiful enough to be cut for Christmas trees, its rot-resistant wood perfect for fence posts. But at some point in the middle of the last century—no one is quite sure when—the trees began to die. Beset by a mysterious disease, overabundant deer, feral hogs, drought, and perhaps a stressful climate, the adult trees were reduced to a handful of mossy trunks, rotting in riverside ravines.

The species persists in Florida as less than a thousand gangly survivors, most only a few feet tall, their trunks no thicker than a child's wrist, none known to reproduce. Much like the American chestnut, these trees are frozen in preadolescence, knocked back by disease or other adversaries before they grow large enough to set seed. To see their grape-size seeds, Barlow had to visit the state park offices, where two sit preserved in a jam jar.

Barlow continued her travels that winter but returned to the park a few years later. She tracked down some of the few remaining trees and, in a quiet moment, sat under one of the largest specimens, perhaps ten feet tall. The Florida torreya, even at its healthiest, isn't an obviously charismatic tree. Its flat needles are scanty; its trunk lacks the grandeur of a redwood or an old-growth fir; when it does manage to produce seeds, the rotting results smell like vomit. In its diminished state, it inspires more pity than awe; to call its spindly limbs a canopy is a sorry joke.

But when Barlow looked up at the branches of the Florida torreya, she made an impulsive commitment to the species. She'd spent years thinking and writing about evolution and ecology, and was aware of the implications of climate change. She decided the species needed to move north, to cooler, less diseased climes. And because it couldn't move fast enough alone, Barlow would move it herself.

Climate change is beginning to make good on its threats, and news of its work is now hard to avoid. Escalating average global temperatures? Check. Rising seas? Check. Plants and animals scampering uphill and toward the poles? Check. Dozens of birds and butterfly species are shifting their ranges to cooler terrain or migrating earlier in the year, each species reacting somewhat differently. Ecological communities, never as stable as we might like to think, are disarticulating in new ways.

Conservationists, in response, have offered more ambitious versions of familiar strategies. Bigger nature reserves. More protected corridors for wildlife migration and movement. More regulations, incentives, and ingenuity in service of greenhouse gas reductions. But even the most expedient tactics could leave some species— especially those as tightly circumscribed as the Florida torreya— marooned in habitat too hot, dry, wet, or stormy.

What then? Captive breeding without hope of reintroduction is an expensive and indefinite custodial project, an ark with no gangplank. The next option sounds either laughable or desperate: pick up the plants and animals, and carry them to better habitat.

Jason McLachlan, an ecologist at the University of Notre Dame, remembers giving a talk in North Carolina about forest responses to climate change. "Someone in the audience said, 'Why is this a problem? You can just move them,'" he says. "I thought he was just being a smartass."

It's an easy idea to caricature. FedEx the polar bears to Antarctica! Airlift the pikas and the orchids! But some scientists take the concept very seriously. Camille Parmesan, a professor at the University of Texas at Austin and an authority on the ecological effects of climate change, remembers broaching the subject at an international conservation conference nearly a decade ago. "I said, 'Look, we need to start thinking about transplanting organisms around these barriers of agricultural land or urban land, and getting them to the next possible suitable habitat as the climate changes,' and people were horrified—just horrified," she says. "They said, 'You can't do that!'"

But discussion continued among scientists—if mostly in whispers—and in 2004, a graduate student named Brian Keel quietly coined a term for the idea: assisted migration. Not long afterward, Connie Barlow and the Florida torreya shoved the debate into the open.

The Apalachicola River is bordered by a thick layer of sand, in places more than a hundred feet deep, left when the sea retreated some two million years ago. Rain—which fell generously here, exceeding sixty inches each year, until the recent drought—hits the loose, sandy soil and keeps going, seeping downward until layers of clay and limestone stop its vertical progress. The moisture then turns toward the main stem of the river, each trickle pulling a few grains of sand with it, a sabotage from below known as sapping erosion.

Over millennia, sapping erosion has created nearly sheer-walled ravines known as steepheads, their sandy banks held in place by magnolias, pines, and muscular beeches. Found in only a handful of other spots throughout the world, steepheads and the shady forests they cradle now define this stretch of the Apalachicola. To step from the sunny, logging-scarred Apalachicola uplands into a steephead is to enter a darker, wetter, more complicated world, ignored by chain saws and seemingly hidden from time.

On a humid fall day near the end of hurricane season, David Printiss leads the way over the edge of a steephead, pointing out the faint, narrow path that hairpins down the wall. A few moments after beginning the descent, he crouches in the leaf litter, then turns with a grin. "Introducing *Torreya taxifolia*!"

The tree is a bundle of pencil-thin stems, the tallest two feet high, ridiculously small in comparison to the mature trees surrounding it, dwarfed even by a single leaf of a nearby needle palm.

Printiss is the manager of this preserve—The Nature Conservancy Apalachicola Bluffs and Ravines Preserve, just south of Torreya State Park—and he's proud that the Florida torreya survives in these ravines, even in this almost symbolic state. But he spends most of his time thinking not about the fewer than a hundred *Torreya taxifolia* on the preserve, but about the landscape surrounding them. Restoring that, he says, is the best way to solve the "Torreya puzzle" and give the tree a chance to thrive.

Printiss has a salt-and-pepper beard, a discreet earring, and a serious demeanor, and he lives here on the preserve with his wife and young daughter. He wears Carhartt work trousers and heavy leather fire boots to the office, and uses both. Each year, he serves as "burn boss" on about twenty prescribed fires, some as large as five hundred acres.

"If I can get fire across the landscape acting in its natural role, I've done my job; I'm home," says Printiss as he drives the soft, sandy roads on the flat preserve uplands. "I'm not saying fire is the answer, but I suspect it's a large part of the answer." Restoring fire to the uplands, he says, thins out the overgrown hardwood trees, makes room for the restoration of longleaf pine stands and native grasslands, and brings some filtered sunlight back to the steep ravines where the Florida torreya once grew.

Printiss acknowledges that even if these efforts were to revive the species, it could still face the perplexing blight, which attacks the trees by killing the stems and leaving the trees to resprout from their bases. Most surviving *Torreya taxifolia*, like the one at Printiss's feet, have withstood multiple onslaughts and are now clusters of genetically identical stems; since the 1960s, only a single tree is known to have set seed. For years, no researcher was able to conclusively identify the disease or its source, and some speculated it might even be a suite of diseases. Only in 2010 was a newly discovered canker, *Fusarium torreyae,* identified as the culprit.

Because *T. taxifolia* has separate male and female plants, any trees that managed to persist through adolescence would need the added good fortune of growing near a mate. Only then could the pollen ride the wind to a female tree and produce the species' distinctively hefty seeds. On top of those difficulties is the Southeast's record-breaking drought, which shrank water supplies to dangerously low levels in the fall of 2007, making the oncoming stresses of climate change difficult to ignore.

Yet the suggestion of assisted migration, of planting *Torreya taxifolia* trees outside these Panhandle steepheads, makes Printiss's face tighten. Such efforts, he says, threaten to take attention and funding away from the work in the preserve, and make an already bad situation even worse.

"A lot of people just want to let it go up there [in Appalachia] and let it rip," he says, his voice rising. "They say it'll act a lot like the northern hemlock, this, that, and the other thing. Yeah, maybe. When it comes to introducing non-native species, we have such overwhelming evidence of good ideas gone bad . . . and this isn't just the Conservancy's policy, it's my personal policy . . . it's very dangerous tinkering.

This is the long-standing conservation credo: with enough space, money, and knowledge, we can protect natural places and, in many cases, restore them by stitching them back together. But though we're welcome to restore, redesign is frowned upon; that sort of tinkering crosses an invisible line between humans and capital-N Nature, and risks making things much worse. We've good reason to distrust ourselves, after all. Until the 1950s, we thought planting kudzu was a good idea.

But climate change calls all this into question. If rising temperatures and changing weather patterns make restoration difficult or impossible, new brands of meddling may sometimes be the only alternative to extinction. Connie Barlow believes *Torreya taxifolia*, with its almost absurdly gloomy prospects in its current range, already requires a new strategy—and she welcomes the chance to provide it.

Barlow describes herself as "more interventionist" than many of the scientists and conservationists she encounters, explaining that her background in ecology and evolutionary biology have immersed her in the long time scales of evolution. "I don't have a sense of what's normal," she says. "I do have a sense of species moving a lot through time."

Following her first visits to Torreya State Park, Barlow started an e-mail correspondence with botanists, conservationists, and others about the future of the tree. Some, such as paleoecologist Paul Martin, loved the idea of moving *T. taxifolia* north. The Florida torreya is widely believed to be an ice age relict, "left behind" after the last glacial retreat and very possibly better suited for cooler climates, with or without global warming. So why not return it to the southern Appalachians, where it grew during the Pleistocene? These arguments were countered by an ecologist named Mark Schwartz, who has studied the Florida torreya at the Apalachicola Bluffs preserve since the late 1980s, and who remains one of the scant handful of scientists with in-depth knowledge of the species. Schwartz defended the chances for restoration in the species' present-day range. Before long, the discussion reached an impasse, and the disagreement found an audience.

In a 2004 forum in the now defunct journal *Wild Earth*, Barlow and Martin made what might be the first public case for assisted migration. Moving even federally endangered plants like the Florida torreya to more favorable climates, they wrote, was "easy, legal, and cheap," and *Torreya taxifolia*, prevented by highways, topography, and its own biology from moving quickly on its own, needed immediate help.

Although horticulturists at the Atlanta Botanical Garden have spent years raising *Torreya taxifolia* in greenhouses and seminatural "potted orchards" in northern Georgia, Barlow and Martin dismissed these efforts, saying that "potted is the botanical equivalent of caged." They proposed that *T. taxifolia* be planted on privately owned forestlands in southern Appalachia, easily four hundred miles from the Florida Panhandle. The risk of the slow-growing, problem-prone Florida torreya becoming an invasive weed is vanishingly small, they argued, and in the Appalachian forests, the tree might even take the place of the eastern hemlock, another subcanopy conifer in precipitous decline.

Schwartz, now a professor at the University of California, Davis, responded by acknowledging both the critical situation of the Florida torreya and the possibility of healthier habitat in Appalachia. But he balked at assisted migration for much the same reasons that David Printiss—and many conservationists of all stripes—meet the idea with almost visceral hostility. The Florida torreya is unlikely to become the next kudzu, but the next species on the poleward wagon might very well prove a nasty invasive. And because scientists don't know precisely what climate change will mean for *Torreya taxifolia* and other species, conservationists can only make rough predictions about future habitats and future relationships among species. The unknowns are staggering.

If the theory of assisted migration isn't controversial enough, Schwartz points out, the reality is sure to be even more contentious: although people may be willing to export familiar species to safer habitats, they're less likely to open their home ecosystems to exotic refugees. "Here in Northern California, if we were to ask people whether we can move a salamander that's going extinct because of climate change into Oregon, people would probably say yes," Schwartz says. "But if we ask people whether we can introduce a Southern California species into a redwood grove for the same reason, they would uniformly say, No way!"

Perhaps the most disturbing implication of assisted migration is that the traditional conservation notion—call it an illusion if you like—of a place to get back to will disappear for good. Yet with or without assisted migration, that pristine place is already slipping out of reach. The demarcation between managed and wild has always been tenuous, defined more by emotion than data, and weakened over decades by the global reach of humankind: acid rain, DDT, PCBs, traces of Prozac in rivers and streams. Climate change is the most dramatic transgression yet, for its effects range from pole to pole and can't be fenced in, mopped up, or halted by a National Park Service boundary.

Climate change is altering the wilderness peak, the backyard nature preserve, the wild and scenic desert river—all the long-standing conservation victories, the places that not only lend inspiration and solace to the conservation movement, but also prove the wisdom of its tactics. In transforming places once thought protected, in violating hard-fought boundaries, climate change is busting the limits of conservation itself.

The passionate critics of assisted migration didn't stop Connie Barlow, who moved briskly ahead with her plans for the Florida torreya. She created a website called the Torreya Guardians, where she and a handful of amateur horticulturists began to trade information about *Torreya taxifolia* cultivation in other habitats.

Their vision of the Florida torreya's future begins in the mountains of north Georgia, where the roads narrow and twist, and travel is measured in time instead of distance. Here, Jack Johnston, a

sleepy-eyed ER nurse and amateur horticulturist, started growing
Florida torreya after meeting Connie Barlow at a dinner in North
Carolina. On the steep ground behind his house, on terraces that
legend has it were used for growing corn for white lightning in the
1930s, Johnston is cultivating a half dozen *Torreya taxifolia* seedlings he bought, legally, from a nursery in South Carolina. Each is
about two feet high, five years old, and healthy.

Johnston, whose isolated property is full of other rare plants ("I'm
moving all sorts of things north," he jokes) is pleased by the apparent flexibility of his charges, and nonchalant about the implications
of assisted migration. "People have been moving plants around for a
long time," he says. "This idea that we should be territorial about our
plants, well, that's just kind of a provincial attitude."

The next day, during a long-awaited rainstorm in western North
Carolina, Lee Barnes, the de facto lieutenant of the Torreya Guardians, is eager to talk Torreya. "I'm a horticulturist," he says. "I'm a
professional tinkerer." Barnes, who is no stranger to *T. taxifolia*—he
wrote his doctoral dissertation in the 1980s on the cultivation of the
Florida torreya and two other endangered Florida species—has so
far collected and distributed about 120 seeds to about a dozen people and gardens north of Georgia, including amateur gardeners in
Ohio, New York, England, Switzerland, and elsewhere. Some recipi-
ents have reported their successes and failures; some have not.

Barnes's seed supply comes from a single grove of *Torreya
taxifolia*, which grows not in Florida but about thirty miles from his
home in North Carolina. In the 1930s and 1940s, on the grounds
of George Vanderbilt's grand Biltmore Estate, an enterprising head
gardener planted seeds he and his botanical accomplices (known
as the Azalea Hunters) collected from throughout the Southeast.

Today, lines of tourists snake through the vast gardens, but few notice the unassuming, thin-limbed conifers that stand, unmarked, among magnolias, pines, oaks, and redwoods.

Bill Alexander, forest historian for the estate, has lived on these grounds for twenty years, and he walks along the curving path through this cultivated forest, pointing out each Florida torreya in turn. These trees, all apparently free of the disease that scourges the Panhandle populations, were likely planted in the 1930s or 1940s—though perhaps as early as the 1890s—and some graze fifty feet, a height now unimaginable in Florida. Despite freezes and hurricanes, the Florida torreya has done itself proud in North Carolina: one of the trees at Biltmore, Alexander believes, is the second largest of the species. The largest stands on a farm in northeastern North Carolina, surrounded by rusting farm equipment.

Alexander, who traces his family back to some of the first European settlers in the Biltmore area, is no ecosaboteur, but he likes the democratic, do-it-yourself approach of the Torreya Guardians, and he wants to see the species survive, no matter its longitude and latitude. He says he'll happily supply seeds to the group as long as the Biltmore trees continue to produce. And if the resulting seedlings establish themselves outside gardens and the manicured grounds of the Biltmore Estate? Alexander looks pleased. "Well," he says, "then I'll think, 'By God, we've been successful.'"

In 2007, ecologist Mark Schwartz and two colleagues, Jessica Hellmann and Jason McLachlan, published a paper that modestly proposed a "framework for debate" on assisted migration. While they criticized "maverick, unsupervised translocation efforts," such as the Torreya Guardians', for their potential to undermine conservation work and create conflict, they directed their harshest criticism at "the far more ubiquitous 'business as usual' scenario that is the current de facto policy." The three scientists take different stands on the notion of assisted migration. All are cautious, but McLachlan is usually the most skeptical, and Hellmann, a University of Notre Dame ecologist who studies butterflies on the northern end of their range in British Columbia, is the most open to the concept. "It's incredibly exciting to think that we could come up with a strategy that might help mitigate the impacts of climate change," she says.

Last fall, to initiate a broader discussion, the three scientists organized a meeting in Davis, California, with other researchers, land managers, environmental groups, and even an environmental ethicist. The Florida torreya isn't the only species that might benefit from immediate assisted migration. The Quino checkerspot butterfly has blinked out on the southern end of its range, in the Mexican state of Baja California, while the northern end of its range, in Southern California, has been transformed by development. In South Africa and Namibia, rising temperatures on the northern edge of the range of the quiver tree are killing the succulent plants before the species has a chance to shift south.

But assisted migration is in no case a clear solution. Beyond initial concerns about new invasive species and territorial conflicts among conservationists, the meeting in California raised new questions: What if assisted migration is used to justify new habitat destruction? Who decides which species are moved, and who moves them? Isn't "assisted colonization" a more appropriate name than "assisted migration," which reminds people of birds on the wing?

Some researchers also worry that continued discussion about the strategy—which most agree is a last resort, likely too expensive and complicated for widespread use—distracts from the more prosaic, immediate duties of conservation and restoration. Brown University ecologist Dov Sax, an invasive-species researcher working on assisted migration, has grander hopes for the conversation. "Conservation has really been built around a static view of the world," he says. "Given that climate change is going to happen, we need a whole new suite of strategies that could complement the old ones. This could get more people thinking about the other strategies we need."

Discussions of climate change always seem to end with a dreary litany of required sacrifices, uncomfortable changes that will be demanded of the penitent. There is no doubt that stabilizing the climate will require deep, societywide reforms, some of them costly. But as climate change delivers its inconvenient truths, it also asks us to chuck a persistent and not-very-useful notion: the idea that conservation, and by extension restoration, is about gilt-framed landscapes.

Commitment to particular places and their histories has taken conservation a long way. It gives conservationists ground to stand on, in ways that range from the literal to the spiritual to the political. And restoring these beloved places to past states can restart ecological processes still relevant to the present day. But this sort of restoration works only when the climate is more or less stable—when the past supplies a reasonable facsimile of the future. Restoration ecologists remind us that the most effective restoration focuses not on a given point in the past, but on the revival of clogged or absent natural processes. When climate change makes historical analogues irrelevant, it's these processes that will help species and systems survive in a new world.

Don Falk, an ecologist at the University of Arizona and the first executive director of the Society for Ecological Restoration, argues that assisted migration is simply another way to impersonate the process of dispersal: its adherents intend to transport species from places humans have made uninhabitable, through places humans have made impassable. Despite its undeniable risks, it may not be as radical as it first seems. It may be just another step in the evolution of conservation.

The job is no longer—if it ever was—to fence off surviving shards of landscape or to try to put everything back the way it used to be. Climate change requires conservationists to husband not a fixed image of a place, but instead the fires, floods, and behaviors that create it, to help species and natural systems respond to a host of changes we're only beginning to understand. Assisted migration is certainly not the right strategy for all species—and given its myriad possible pitfalls, it may not be the right choice for any species. Yet the idea of it and the discussion it provokes point toward the future.

Mark Schwartz, for his part, still holds out hope for the recovery of the Florida torreya in Florida, for a small but healthy population of trees in the shady steephead ravines. But each time he visits the Panhandle, he says, he sees fewer and fewer *Torreya taxifolia*.

AFAA MICHAEL WEAVER

Leaves

The lines that make you are infinite, but I count them
every day to hear the stories you carry. These are not secrets
but records, things we should know but ignore. If I commit
the sin of tearing you from the tree, I find another world
inside the torn vein, another lifetime of counting the records
of who walked here before, of what lovers lay here
holding each other through wars and starvation.

Some days I stand here until I lose focus and travel,
drifting off out of the moment, too full of it, and my legs
are now like trees, mindless but vigilant, held
into the earth by the rules of debt, what we owe
to nature for trying to tear ourselves away. I drift
and the pleasure of touch comes again, layers of green
in the mountainside a tickling in my palms.

The pleasure is that of being lost here in the crowd
of trunks and pulp, the ground thick with the death of you,
sinking under my feet as I go, touching one and another,
linking myself through until the place where I entered
is gone. When I am afraid, my breath is caught in my throat.
When I am not afraid, I lift both hands up under a bunch
of you to find the way the world felt on the first day.

BIOGRAPHIES

Rick Bass, a National Book Critics Circle Award finalist for his memoir *Why I Came West*, was born and raised in Texas, worked as a petroleum geologist in Mississippi, and has lived in Montana's Yaak Valley for almost three decades. He is the writer in residence at Montana State University.

Andrea Cohen's poems have appeared in *The New Yorker*, *Poetry*, *The Threepenny Review*, *The Atlantic*, and elsewhere. Her seventh collection, *Everything*, was recently published by Four Way Books. "First Thought, Best Thought" has appeared in Cohen's book *Furs Not Mine* (Four Way Books, 2015).

Alison Hawthorne Deming is a poet, essayist, and teacher, former Agnese Nelms Haury Chair in Environment and Social Justice and currently Regents Professor in Creative Writing at the University of Arizona. "The Web" has appeared in Deming's book *Rope* (2009), published by Penguin Press.

Leslie Harrison holds graduate degrees from the Johns Hopkins University and the University of California, Irvine. Her first book, *Displacement*, won the Bakeless Prize and was published by Mariner Books. She lives and teaches in Baltimore.

John Hay (1915–2011) was the author of *The Run* and *The Great Beach*, among other noteworthy books. He was a naturalist, conservation activist, and one of the founders of the Cape Cod Museum of Natural History in Brewster, Massachusetts.

Lilah Hegnauer lives with her family in Massachusetts, where she works as an obstetric nurse. She has been honored with residencies at the Amy Clampitt House and the MacDowell Colony, and has also taught poetry at the University of Virginia, Sweet Briar College, and James Madison University.

Robin Wall Kimmerer is a mother, scientist, decorated professor, and enrolled member of the Citizen Potawatomi Nation. She is the author of *Braiding Sweetgrass: Indigenous Wisdom, Scientific Knowledge, and the Teachings of Plants* and *Gathering Moss: A Natural and Cultural History of Mosses*. She lives in Syracuse, New York, where she is a SUNY distinguished teaching professor of environmental biology, and founder and director of the Center for Native Peoples and the Environment.

Dorianne Laux is the author of several collections of poetry. She has received fellowships from the Guggenheim Foundation and the National Endowment for the Arts, and has been a Pushcart Prize winner. Her last full-length book, *Only As the Day Is Long*, was a finalist for the Pulitzer Prize. "Roots" was featured in *The Book of Men: Poems* (2011, W. W. Norton & Company).

Jessica J. Lee is a British-Canadian-Taiwanese author, environmental historian, and winner of the 2019 RBC Taylor Prize Emerging Writer Award. She is the author of *Turning* and *Two Trees Make a Forest*, short-listed for the 2020 Weston Writers' Trust Prize for Nonfiction. She has a PhD in environmental history and aesthetics, and is founding editor of *The Willowherb Review* and a researcher at the University of Cambridge.

Ursula K. Le Guin (1929–2018) was a celebrated and beloved author of twenty-one novels, eleven volumes of short stories, four collections of essays, twelve children's books, six volumes of poetry, and four works in translation. The breadth and imagination of her work earned her six Nebulas, nine Hugos, and SFWA's Grand Master, along with the PEN/Malamud and many other awards. In 2014, she was awarded the National Book Foundation Medal for Distinguished Contribution to American Letters, and in 2016 joined the short list of authors to be published in their lifetimes by the Library of America.

William Bryant Logan is founder and president of Urban Arborists and is on the faculty of the New York Botanical Garden. His four books of nonfiction have all been published by W. W. Norton & Company, one of which became an award-winning documentary. "The Things Trees Know" won the 2020 Nature Essay Award of the John Burroughs Association and originally appeared in *Sprout Lands: Tending the Endless Gift of Trees* (W. W. Norton & Company, 2019).

Robin MacArthur lives with her husband and two young children on the Vermont hillside where she was born. She won the PEN/New England Award for fiction in 2016 and has been a finalist for the Vermont Book Award and a two-time finalist for the New England Book Award.

Terese Mailhot is the author of *Heart Berries*, a finalist for the Governor General's Literary Award for English-language nonfiction. She is the recipient of a Whiting Award and the Spalding Prize for the Promotion of Peace and Justice in Literature. She teaches creative writing at Purdue University and Vermont College of Fine Arts.

Emma Marris is a nonfiction writer based in Oregon. Her work has appeared in *National Geographic*, the *New York Times*, *The Atlantic*, *Wired*, *Outside*, *High Country News*, and *Nature*, among others. Her second book, *Wild Souls: Freedom and Flourishing in the Non-Human World*, was published in 2021.

Adrian Matejka was born in Nuremberg, Germany, and grew up in Indiana. He is the author of five books, most recently *Somebody Else Sold the World* (Penguin, 2021). He teaches at Indiana University in Bloomington.

Michelle Nijhuis is the author of the book *Beloved Beasts: Fighting for Life in an Age of Extinction*. A project editor for *The Atlantic* and a longtime contributing editor for *High Country News*, she writes about science and the environment for *National Geographic* and other publications.

Cecily Parks is at work on a third book of poetry, poems from which appear in *The New Yorker, Best American Poetry 2020, Best American Poetry 2021,* and elsewhere. She teaches in the MFA program at Texas State University. "Bell" appears in her book *O'Nights* (Alice James Books, 2015).

Lucia Maria Perillo (1958–2016) was an American poet. In 2000, Perillo was recognized with a "genius grant" as part of the MacArthur Fellows Program.

Michael Pollan is the author of seven books, all of which were *New York Times* bestsellers. A longtime contributor to *The New York Times Magazine,* he also teaches writing at Harvard and the University of California, Berkeley. In 2010, *TIME* magazine named him one of the one hundred most influential people in the world.

Richard Preston is a bestselling author of ten books, nonfiction and fiction, whose works reveal hidden worlds of nature and wonder. Preston is a contributor to *The New Yorker,* and all of his nonfiction books have first appeared as articles there.

Lia Purpura's *On Looking* (essays) was a finalist for the National Book Critics Circle Award. *It Shouldn't Have Been Beautiful* (poems) and *All the Fierce Tethers* (essays) are her most recent collections. A Guggenheim Fellow, Purpura is writer in residence at the University of Maryland, Baltimore County.

Alberto Álvaro Ríos is an academic and author of ten books and chapbooks of poetry, three collections of short stories, and a memoir. In August 2013, Ríos was named Arizona's first state poet laureate, a position he held until 2015.

Scott Russell Sanders is the author of more than twenty books of fiction and nonfiction, including *Hunting for Hope* and *A Conservationist Manifesto*. His latest book, *The Way of Imagination*, was published in 2020 by Counterpoint Press. An emeritus professor of English at Indiana University, he lives in the hardwood hill country of the Ohio Valley. "Buckeye" was collected in *Writing from the Center* (Indiana University Press, 1995).

Julia Shipley is an independent journalist and the author of *The Academy of Hay*, winner of the 2014 Melissa Lanitis Gregory Poetry Prize, and *Adam's Mark*, named a Best Book of 2014 by the *Boston Globe*.

Robert Sullivan is the author of *Rats*, *The Meadowlands*, *A Whale Hunt*, and *The Thoreau You Don't Know*. His writing has appeared in *The New Yorker*, the *New York Times*, *New York*, *A Public Space*, *Condé Nast Traveler, GQ,*, and *Vogue*, where he is a contributing editor. He lives in New York.

Arthur Sze is a poet, translator, and editor. He has published eleven collections of poetry, including *Sight Lines*, which received the 2019 National Book Award for Poetry, and *The Glass Constellation: New and Collected Poems* (Copper Canyon Press, 2021).

Geronimo G. Tagatac has published numerous short stories in literary journals. His short story collection, *The Weight of the Sun*, was a 2007 Oregon Literary Arts Award finalist. His story "Summer of the Aswang" won the *Timberline Review*'s Short Story Award in 2017. Geronimo is the son of a Filipino immigrant father and a Russian Jewish mother.

Joni Tevis is the author of two collections of essays: *The World Is on Fire: Scrap, Treasure, and Songs of Apocalypse* and *The Wet Collection: A Field Guide to Iridescence and Memory*. A winner of a National Endowment for the Arts Fellowship, she serves as the Bennette Geer Associate Professor of English at Furman University in Greenville, South Carolina.

Katrina Vandenberg is the author of *The Alphabet Not Unlike the World* and *Atlas*. She is a professor in the creative writing program at Hamline University.

Afaa Michael Weaver is a poet, short story writer, and editor. His recent book of poetry is *Spirit Boxing*. He has received a Fulbright, a Guggenheim Fellowship, multiple Pushcarts, and other awards. "Leaves" appeared in Weaver's *The Government of Nature* (University of Pittsburgh Press, 2013), winner of the 2014 Kingsley Tufts Award. He teaches at Sarah Lawrence College.

ABOUT *ORION* MAGAZINE

Orion is a nonprofit, ad-free, quarterly magazine whose mission is to invite readers into a community of caring for the planet. Since its first issue was published in 1982, *Orion* has sought to explore and enrich the mysterious connections between people and the environments we inhabit, inspiring new thinking about how humanity might live on Earth justly, sustainably, and joyously.

Contributing Editors
John Freeman, Ross Gay, Amy Irvine, J. Drew Lanham,
Sy Montgomery, Aimee Nezhukumatathil, Emily Raboteau,
Elizabeth Rush, Meera Subramanian

Advisors
Jad Abumrad, Wendell Berry, Eula Biss, David James Duncan,
Jane Goodall, Jane Hirshfield, Linda Hogan, Elizabeth Kolbert,
Fiona McCrae, Bill McKibben, Lulu Miller, Michael Pietsch,
Michael Pollan, Mary Roach, Scott Russell Sanders, Paul Slovak,
Gary Snyder, Rebecca Solnit, Rob Spillman, Sandra Steingraber,
Krista Tippett, Mary Evelyn Tucker, Luis Alberto Urrea,
Edward O. Wilson

Print or digital subscriptions can be purchased at www.orion magazine.org, where you can also find posters, tote bags, and other merchandise. Visit www.orionmagazine.org/workshops for information about virtual and in-person opportunities to share your own work with award-winning authors.

The work featured in this volume was made possible by generous donations from readers and foundations. To learn how you can support *Orion*, visit www.orionmagazine.org/donate, e-mail development@orionmagazine.org, or call (888) 909-6568 ext. 14.

More books from *Orion* magazine

To Eat with Grace
Animals & People
Leave No Child Inside
Wonder and Other Survival Skills
Change Everything Now
Thirty-Year Plan
Beyond Ecophobia
Place-Based Education
Earthly Love
The Most Radical Thing You Can Do